W.B. Wollen
1881

PAGEANTRY OF SPORT

1st endpaper An American ten-pin
bowling alley: a ladies' game, played
in 1872.

2nd endpaper Football: a maul in goal,
by W. B. Wollen, 1881.

3rd endpaper Hawking, by T. Morris,
published in 1780.

1. The Cumberland Sailing Society,
by J. Kitchingame, engraved by
B. Pouncey and published in 1778.

The Meeting of the Royal British Bowmen

PAGEANTRY OF SPORT

FROM THE AGE OF CHIVALRY TO THE AGE OF VICTORIA

by John Arlott and Arthur Daley

With selections from the writings of William Hazlitt, Pierce Egan, Nimrod, Izaak Walton,
Mark Twain, Henry Fielding, Charles Dickens and many others

Illustrated with 16 colour plates and 144 contemporary drawings, engravings and paintings

PAUL ELEK PRODUCTIONS
London

Published in Great Britain by Paul Elek Productions Ltd 2 All Saints Street London N1

General Editors: Paul and Elizabeth Elek

Anthology collected and selected by Terence Delaney

Illustrations collected by Prue Sykes

Design and typography by Harold Bartram

Pageantry of Sport © Paul Elek Productions Ltd 1968

Pageantry of Sport by John Arlott © Paul Elek Productions Ltd 1968

The American Scene © Paul Elek Productions Ltd 1968

Filmset in England by The Birmingham Typesetters Ltd

Printed in Italy by Amilcare Pizzi S.p.A.

2. *Previous page* Hawking, from the *Queen Mary Psalter*, c. 1310.

3. Winter fishing for pickerel in North America, 1872.

Frontispiece THE MEETING OF THE ROYAL BRITISH BOWMEN IN THE GROUNDS OF ERTHIG, DENBIGHSHIRE, THE SEAT OF SIMON YORKE, ESQ, ON SEPTEMBER 13TH, 1822.

From a drawing by J. Townsend, engraved by Bennett, and coloured by W. H. Timms
24ins × 17½ins

Erthig (or Erddig) Hall stands on the ancient rampart called Wat's Dyke, once a boundary between England and Wales, and near it is a pre-Roman camp. This suggestion of the historic past no doubt appealed to those early 19th century romantics who revived the old and serious craft of archery as a fashionable pastime for ladies and gentlemen. 'In these days of refinement' wrote Pierce Egan, 'when the recreations of the wealthier orders are too often luxurious and enervating, and when their semi-foreign habits of life have too much estranged them from the interchange of domestic hospitalities, we hail with pleasure a rural and elegant amusement, having a strong tendency to correct both these evils.'

'It is not everyone,' he points out, 'that can conveniently give an Archery Meeting. Two things are indispensable – a fortune able to bear the expense, and a park, or other grounds, favourable to the purpose; and such members as are without these advantages are not expected to give one. A uniform is appointed, which is always (to our knowledge) green, but may vary in minor points according to the caprices of fashion or taste; and those members who do not appear in it are fined. It is this costume that chiefly imparts the characteristic and beautiful appearance to the scene, which it must be allowed to possess, especially if laid in some wild and romantic park. It is then and there that the lover of antiquity might muse on ancestral times, and fancy that they were again about to return. The evening is generally concluded by a ball, which need only be mentioned as differing from other balls with respect to the costume of the assembled party; but that circumstance gives to it a very unique and pleasing appearance. Of course, as in all such out-of-door amusements, much depends upon the weather; but when that is favourable, it may easily be conceived to be a scene of much pleasure and animation.'

CONTENTS

4. Sea bathing in the 1820s. The
bathing machine in this drawing was
a wooden wagon invented by Benjamin
Beale. It was pulled into the sea by
horses, and allowed the bathers some
privacy while taking their dip.

1. HUNTERS ON THEIR WAY TO THE HUNTING STABLES

*From a print after James Pollard, engraved by H. Pyall, and published in 1829 by
Thos. McLean, London, and Giraldon Bovinet, Paris.* 17½ins × 14ins

James Pollard was the son of Robert Pollard, draughtsman, engraver and publisher –
a Newcastle man who came to London in 1782 and was one of the founders of the
Artists' Benevolent Fund. James took up his father's trade, and pictures by him
were exhibited at the Royal Academy in 1821, 1824 and 1839. The greater part of
his work had to do with coaching – the coaches themselves, the roads, the dilemmas
of the coachmen, horses and passengers, rainstorms and snowstorms, and the inns
that marked the stages of the journeys. Here is a characteristic English country scene
that, excepting the clothes, might be duplicated today: the gentlemen huntsmen on
their way home, the innkeeper's wife, the servant holding the horses, home brewed
ale for the road, and, in the background, a typical Pollard evening sky with a
suggestion of moisture in the air.

SPIRITS

HOME BREWD ALE *DEALER IN* FOREIGN

J.ˢ HALL

JAMES POLLARD, *Pinxit.*

HUNTERS on their way to the HUNTING STABLES.

H PYALL, *Sculpsit.*

LIST OF PLATES

– certainly not when his work may make the difference between life and death by starvation in the following winter. A peasantry sufficiently solvent to enjoy fifty-six days a year of holiday no more existed in medieval England than it has ever done in any period or country.

In the nineteenth century the Industrial Revolution, with its savagely long hours of exhausting work, unhealthy housing conditions and low subsistence levels, shackled men. It not only restricted their leisure time, but left them with little strength for games. It is not always remembered that the idea of a free Saturday afternoon for workers was not generally accepted until the Act of 1863, and then by no means in all industries: that paid holidays for the working class were unheard of until relatively recent days: that a hundred years ago, children of ten and eleven were worked to death in vile conditions and women were used to drag coal trucks in the mines. Even in recent years, miners, day after day, went down the pit before break of day and did not come up again until after darkness had fallen. On a milder plane it is still accepted automatically in many village cricket clubs that farm workers are not available for matches during harvest time.

Yet man is flexible: his spirit is, ultimately, unquenchable. It may be argued that simple hunger dictated flouting of the game laws: but certainly ordinary working Englishmen, at different periods, persisted with football, cards, quoits, bowls, boxing and cock-fighting in defiance of the law. The serfs of the Middle Ages, on Sundays and Saints' Days when they could be free, danced, sang and played their primitive games with zest and humour. Out of the coal mines and the 'dark satanic mills' of nineteenth-century industry came the fine cricketers of Yorkshire, Lancashire, Notts and Derbyshire. The coalfields and shipyards of the North-East bred generations of handball players who, even if their fame was only local, were considerable athletes: and from those areas, Scotland and the Midlands came the early professional footballers who created fresh techniques and standards.

In the course of history, too, vital changes took place in the focal points, and patronage, of sport. The rich man's amusements might be centred on the court or his, and his fellows', estates. But for the poor the Church was, for many years, the hub of life, not only of worship, but of free time and of pleasures. In the fourteenth century, for instance, a parish record notes, without comment, that a man was paid 'Four pence for making clean the church against the day of drinking in the said church'. Much of the play on feast days took place within the churchyard and, until the power of the Puritans mounted, there was dancing and singing in the church itself.

As the common people lost many of their holy day holidays to legislation by Henry VIII, and Sunday sport and recreation within the church precincts were banned by the Puritans, they moved out to the village green, sometimes to the patronage of the squire or local lord and, eventually, into independence in their own fields. Meanwhile, sport from the higher social levels, still retaining its privileges, filtered down through the public schools, the universities and the clubs, to the point where, in 1882, Old Etonians met – and, incidentally, beat – Blackburn Rovers in the Final of the F.A. Cup at Kennington Oval.

So far as the mass of the English people are concerned, their actual play falls into five distinct historic periods. The first is that of the Roman occupation, when manly pursuits designed to improve military standards – running and all kinds of physical combat, from wrestling and boxing through to gladiatorial combats to the death – were organized at many levels and presented as spectacles in an age which, in Juvenal's words, 'limits its people's anxious longings to two things only – bread and the games of the circus'.

Then came the long period when, in an England where the Roman roads fell into disrepair, most of the people lived in small, isolated villages, and amused themselves on holy days. These amusements were not all active. The mummers, minstrels, actors (especially in the miracle and morality plays), singers and story-tellers entertained them: there was dancing and singing: and the young ran and played simple, basic games which were the origin of most of those we play today.

Side by side with these diversions, however, there grew up

10. Queen Elizabeth I was a keen patron of stag-hunting, which was, in the 16th century, still a royal sport. It was the custom to present the knife to the most distinguished follower of the hunt to deliver the death-blow, and in this contemporary woodcut Elizabeth takes the knife from the kneeling courtier.

If on your man you light
The first draught shall you play,
If not 'tis mine by right
At first to lead the way

11. Frontispiece to *The Famous Game of Chess* by A. Saul, 1614.

the imposed practice of archery which developed the skill with the long bow that was to make England a victorious military power. Some writers have included hunting – especially coursing – among the amusements of the medieval people. But it is hard to believe that hunting was a diversion for them in face of the brutal game laws of their time. Their entire economic and social background argues that they hunted – legally speaking, poached – in order to eat fresh meat when they would otherwise have had salt meat or none at all.

With the Tudors and Stuarts, urban games established an independent course. Gambling grew more widespread: spectator sports increased, including savage sports such as bear-baiting, bull-baiting and cock-fighting, while mob-football irritated, and sometimes frightened, the middle class and middle-aged.

Gradually over the next two centuries a series of sporting monarchs proved sympathetic to the amusements of their people. We may quote James I (*Book of Sports*): 'Our pleasure is that, after the end of Divine Service, Our good people be not disturbed, letted or discouraged from any lawful recreation, such as dancing, either of men or women, archery for men, leaping, vaulting, nor from having of May games, Whitson Ales, morris dances or the setting up of Maypoles in due and convenient time without impediment or neglect of Divine Service, and women shall have leave to carry rushes to Church for the decorating of it according to the old custom'.

All this led on steadily to the 'sporting' days of the Regency. In that period the young aristocrats generally referred to as the 'Bucks' turned full-bloodedly to every sort of sporting pleasure, extravagance and contest. It was a period of vast wagering and all the sharp practice – indeed, as was frankly stated, cheating and bribery – that high bets invariably breed. The rich had long enjoyed their own privileged sports such as hunting, riding, jousting, tennis and bowls. But now these young men extended the range in all directions. There were brilliant performers among the gifted amateurs and even more

among the professionals – jockeys, boxers, cricketers, pedestrians and wrestlers – whom the 'bloods' employed and backed. If much of the sport of this time was tainted, nevertheless it produced a remarkably high standard of ability which was to provide the springboard for the following stage of development.

This was a characteristically Victorian phenomenon: but, once that is said, all that follows is complex. There existed from the Georgian and Regency times a vein of competence far stronger than that of the folk and village games which still existed, but were now overshadowed. Progress took place simultaneously on many planes. A series of benevolent autocrats addressed themselves seriously, and successfully, to correcting abuses and corruption in a number of major sports. Undergraduates at Oxford and Cambridge, sons, actual or spiritual, of the 'Bucks', widened the range of sports played at the Universities. The growth in the number of public schools, which doubled in number during the nineteenth century, was another important factor. The attitude of which Arnold of Rugby was the exemplar, but shared by many other Victorian headmasters of the chief boarding schools – *mens sana in corpore sano* – produced a hitherto unimagined outflow of boys and young men who had been trained, often by professional coaches, to play a number of sports to a new high level of proficiency. In many cases – notably football and cricket – they served as missionaries, spreading skill in those games through their home towns and villages during their vacations and in their after-school life. Almost entirely from this source came the new, in fact revolutionary, concept of 'sportsmanship' – fair play – with its various aspects of magnanimity in victory, graciousness in defeat and refusal to take any advantage of an opponent which might seem at all unfair – a code which, at times, led to almost absurd lengths of quixotry, but which also saved many games from excessive bitterness. A third powerful influence was the growth of working-class organizations; if the Mechanics' Institutes were the most powerful, they were not alone, for numerous Church clubs existed, drawing young men together and organizing games for them. The reduction of privilege gave men and boys of the working class new opportunities to state their wishes, and the legislation passed, albeit slowly, to restrict working hours gave them increased leisure for games. Finally, the coming of the railways and general improvement in communications extended the range of competition.

These advances were reflected in four important ways, quite apart from the steady improvement in performance. Crowds, and the entire idea of spectatorship, increased greatly and rapidly. Professionalism was extended to more sports. Serious organization and standardization followed and, in the last half of the nineteenth century, various bodies of honorary well-wishers of their particular sports formulated the rules which still substantially govern their conduct all over the world. Above all, there was a vast democratization of those sports which were not strictly confined to those of ample financial resources. At first in cricket, football and athletics, the upper and lower classes began to play together with steadily decreasing regard for strictly *class* differences. On the other hand, a fresh and equally rigid distinction was established – that between amateur and professional. Finally, the idea spread of international competition – and of World Championships.

The spread of British games and equally, if less obviously, of British standards of behaviour in those games was all but automatic, because of the extent of the British Empire in the nineteenth century. For this reason cricket, for instance, took firm root not only in the countries now well known for the game, such as Australia, South Africa, India – and subsequently Pakistan – New Zealand and the West Indies, but also in Ceylon, Fiji and, not negligibly, Singapore, Hong Kong and Central Africa.

Gradually during the nineteenth century the attitude, first of the United States of America – formerly a British colony, speaking the same language and with a substantial proportion of its population of British origin – and then of a number of European nations shifted from disinterest often bordering on contempt towards the British ideas on competitive sport.

Subsequently Britain has been beaten at most sports by many of those countries. So, though not the major power in those fields at the moment, Britain provides the foundation of any history of virtually all of them.

By 1900 all this was achieved, and modern sport was created. Subsequent changes have been largely of degree.

Looking back at the history of games in England, it is striking how few of them have died out. Some, certainly, have merged into others; there have been those which, largely artificial, have boomed and disappeared as phases of fashion, while another group has been killed by the growth of humane principles. On the whole, however, they have developed healthily, from herbs of the field to highly developed, cultivated and trained blooms of athleticism.

For the purposes of this book we are not concerned with the various entertainments from the mumming and dancing of early times to the more sophisticated circuses, fairs, pleasure gardens and 'spectacles' which lack the competitive element. Our interest is in the body of what is now generally called 'sport' – a word which existed in no other language except English, but now has been adopted into many.

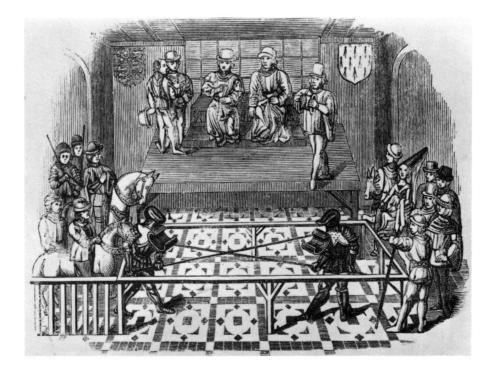

12. *Left* Tilting match between Nick Clifford and J. Boucwell, from *Froissart's Chronicles*, 14th century.

13. *Above* Hawking: late 16th century cushion cover.

We may look at their widely differing histories under nine heads – Warlike Pursuits; Self-defence; The Chase; Folk Games; Baiting; Horse Sports; Water Sports; Athletics; Ball Games.

WARLIKE PURSUITS

The Roman occupation of Britain was essentially military. In terms of weather, natural resources and culture, the country had little to tempt people accustomed to Italy to settle there with pleasure. So the sports the Romans practised in England were organized with a view to improving military efficiency – running, boxing, spear-throwing, horsemanship, wrestling, sword-play and – which was almost to die out in England for centuries after the Romans left – swimming. The climax of their entertainments was usually a gladiatorial fight, either against animals or between men. The gladiators were often slaves, fighting for their lives and, perhaps, freedom, which was sometimes granted to the more successful. Life was never again quite so cheap in England.

It may be that the Romans left behind them traces of their sports in a primitive form of hurling with a religious origin, and a game akin to golf. Their civilization and their games, however, like their roads, were soon overgrown by the totally foreign pattern of Saxon life.

The Romans, it seems, were indifferent archers, but there is evidence that the short bow was in use in Saxon England; and it was employed by horsemen on both sides at the Battle of Hastings. During the next century the long (six foot) yew bow was developed concentratedly in England, and archery, under persuasion amounting often to compulsion, became a 'sport' of the common people. The crossbow, regarded as a less efficient weapon, was banned in England, though for some centuries it was employed by poachers.

Archery was, above all, an effective way of winning battles. It was already a well-established skill before the Statute of Winchester (1285) decreed that every Englishman who was

14. *Above* Frontispiece by John June to *The Art of Angling* by R. Brookes, 1740.

15. *Right A Grand Shooting Match, 1583.* On 17th September, 3000 London archers held a Grand Shooting Match. They marched through the streets of London, accompanied by bellmen, footmen and pages, to Hodgson's Field, in Shoreditch. Later the victors were carried home by torchlight to a banquet at the palace of the Bishop of London.

not a measurable land-owner must keep a bow – later required to be of his own height – and that every town must build butts where the archers were bound to practise on the Sabbath and Holy Days. Archery was not only compulsory, but protected. A variety of ordinances forbade many other games, not because it was felt that there was any inherent evil in them, but because they might keep men from archery. So the yews grew in English churchyards and Englishmen, by competitive practice, became such masters of the longbow that Bishop Latimer, in an 'official policy' sermon described their archery as 'a gift of God that he hath given us to excell all other nations: it hath been God's instrument whereby he hath given us victories against our enemies.'

By the mid-seventeenth century, the introduction of fire-arms into war reduced the importance of archery. It was long maintained, however, on a high social level as a pastime and, in Victorian times, the Queen allowed the Toxophilite Society to use the prefix 'Royal'. Anyone who has shot with a full length bow will have been amazed by its power – which must be seen to be believed – and by the precision a skilled archer can attain.

The sporting glory of medieval times, however, was the tournament, which originated in France but was adopted with immense enthusiasm in England where it afforded the most gallant and colourful spectacle the country has ever known. A more romantic form of the rather idealistic 'aristocratic' wars of the time, and limited to those of noble blood – no one below the rank of Esquire could enter the arena – it was the visible flowering of the concept of 'chivalry'. The tournament took a number of forms, or ingredients. In its 'purest' form, two mounted knights in armour jousted – charged and attempted to unhorse one another with their lances. But often teams of knights would engage in a mêlée and the encounter might be settled on foot, with swords. The lances were usually blunted but in some 'blood' contests they were not: their swords, too, were lethal and, for all the bright fancy of his lady's favour on his helmet, it was not unknown for a knight to be killed in the combat. The whole setting of

the tournament, with its elaborate trappings, banners, tents, daïses, pavilions, the complicated rules of contest and etiquette – amounting virtually to ritual – the spectators of both sexes, the feasting and the lordly entertainments, made a lushly elaborate occasion, which frequently continued for several days.

John Stow notes, too, that in the sixteenth century the young men of London, 'courtiers' and 'attendants of noblemen' – but clearly excluding the nobility – practised 'feats of warre' on horseback and on foot in the fields outside the city.

16. *Trap ball played at the Black Prince, Newington,* drawn and engraved by Bowles and Carver, 1738. Trap ball was an early ball-game: its rules are uncertain, but it probably had a considerable influence on cricket.

In a simpler form there was tilting at a quintain – in which the horseman charged at a weighted dummy: if he hit the target truly, all was well: if he did not, the sandbag with which it was counter-weighted would swing round and unhorse him. This sport did not remain the pursuit of the nobles but, with its opposite poles of success and ridicule, it passed into the common life and at village fairs, Whitson Ales, or wedding feasts the contestants would charge it on foot or in boats, when a ducking was the penalty for inaccuracy.

Much of medieval swordsmanship tended towards crudity; the double-handed sword was as cumbersome as it was deadly. But sword and buckler contests – using a light, one-handed sword in attack and a small round shield for defence – remained both popular and dangerous for some centuries, particularly in London where fights between experts drew large audiences. Unfortunately the 'sport' bred a race of swaggerers and bullies, and at one period it was forbidden by law.

Fencing – taught in fashionable schools according to continental methods – became popular in England in Elizabethan times. For all that some traditionalists condemned it as 'unmanly', its delicate skill and, at need, its effectively lethal quality, established it, and threw up another group of braggadoccios who in many cases did not hesitate to kill.

Quarter staff, in which men contended with six-foot poles held in the centre with one hand and near the end with the other, was a hearty, if not gentle, sport popular in the country and scientifically taught in towns until far into the Tudor period.

Rifle shooting has never become a truly popular sport outside service circles. Modern war, in simple fact, can offer no such attractions or delights as the tournaments of old: war has become war.

SELF-DEFENCE

The eighteenth-century teachers of 'The Noble Art of Self Defence' did not confine their instruction to boxing, but included wrestling, quarter-staff, broadsword and cudgel.

2. AN HOLLAND SMOCK

to be run for by any woman in this county; the best woman in three heats.
N.B. The runners will be entered by the Clerk of the Course before starting, and after the race; cocking as usual.

From a print after John Collett, published in 1770 by Robert Sayer and John Smith, London.
$13\frac{7}{8}$ins × $9\frac{3}{4}$ins

With donkey racing, climbing a greasy pole for a leg of mutton and jumping in sacks, this running for a smock, or shift, was one of the traditional English rural sports, and was common at country fairs and feasts in many parts of England. It was originally part of the rustic celebrations of Ascension Day in the North. Such celebrations usually went along with heavy eating and drinking, and were considered vulgar and indelicate by a higher class of people. The girls ran in their chemises, and the winner was expected to wear her prize as soon as the race was over. Pierce Egan records the case of a young woman who refused to do so on the grounds that a shift was an inner garment. The judges applauded her modesty, and allowed her, against ancient custom, to walk off with the garment under her arm.

In Collett's picture, one barefoot woman is just completing the race, while another, behind her, has tripped over a dog, and is being helped to her feet by a spectator. The course is enclosed by ropes, which hold back the jostling crowd, and some onlookers have climbed on to a waggon to catch a better view. On the left the men are more interested in their beer than the race, but a boy up a tree is enthusiastically waving a shirt and two caps. The notice nailed to the tree reads 'To be run for by men in sacks. A flitch of bacon. On Tuesday next.' It is a picture of true village life, steeped in coarse gaiety and abundant ale.

17. *Above* Woodcut of an angler, from the *Book of St. Albans* by Dame Juliana Berners, 1486. Dame Berners was the Lady Prioress of Sopwell nunnery, in Hertfordshire, and was celebrated for her beauty and learning. Her book, properly entitled *The Book of Hawking, Hunting and Blasing of Arms*, with a *Treatyse of Fysshinge* added in 1496, is one of the earliest printed books in the English language.

18. *Right* A woodcut of fencing in the 17th century.

An Holland Smock

The Romans had known the cestus – a leather or metal 'glove' of murderous effect – but for centuries afterwards boxing was a crude, bare-fist sport of rustic festivals. Wrestling, on the other hand, developed genuine traditions and in Cumberland, Westmorland, Devon and Cornwall positive schools of method emerged and the local champions enjoyed considerable standing into modern times. In London, too, there were organized wrestling matches between teams as early as 1222.

There is a record of a boxing booth in London, and of a boxing match in Hyde Park, quite early in the eighteenth century. Those boxers, however, seem to have fought without rules; often they introduced bludgeons into the contest.

In 1719, a certain James Figg, proprietor of an 'Academy of Boxing', declared himself Champion of England, and defended that title for many years. Suddenly boxing became fashionable.

One of Figg's pupils, John Broughton, who became Champion of England in 1740, opened an ambitious amphitheatre in Tottenham Court Road from which, in 1743, he issued the first 'Rules to be Observed in all Battles on the Stage'. Only one of them, however, restricted the methods of the fighters once they were 'fairly set-to' – 'No person is to hit his Adversary when he is down, or seize him by the ham, the breeches, or any part below the waist'. Otherwise, all was fair, including throws and trips, and the winner was the man whose opponent could not be brought to 'toe the line' within half a minute of being put down.

Broughton introduced the use of padded gloves, but only for practice bouts. There followed a period in which boxing, although illegal, was so immensely popular that few magistrates dared enforce the law forbidding it. A long succession of picturesque characters – Slack, Hen Pearce (the Game Chicken), Mendoza, Gentleman Jackson, Tom Cribb, Tom Spring, Ward, Molyneaux, Bendigo, Belcher, Gully and scores more whose names and performances are vividly recorded in Pierce Egan's *Boxiana* – fought the savage bare-knuckle battles which form the history of the Prize Ring. For

fear of legal intervention, their fights would be arranged for some 'secret' rendezvous, but the secret was so open that hours before they began the 'Fancy' and the populace would be on the way to watch. Often the fighters stood toe to toe for several hours, battering at one another with fists pickled in brine, bleeding and all but insensible on their feet, until one or the other could not 'come up to the mark'. Many of the champions of those days made small fortunes – and, in most cases, lost them – but the sums they earned by their amazing endurance were nothing by comparison with the amounts won by their backers.

In 1860 Tom Sayers, a former bricklayer and the undisputed Champion of England, was challenged by an American, John Heenan. Although the Chief Constable of Hertfordshire applied for a warrant for their arrest to prevent the fight, he was less well informed than the boxing enthusiasts. The two fighters set off in the opposite direction and, a few minutes before half-past-seven in the morning of 17 April 1860, they began their fight in a well protected and thickly crowded field at Farnborough in Hampshire. Heenan – 'The Benicia Boy' – was six inches taller and two stones heavier than his opponent and part way through the fight – following a round which lasted a quarter hour when the two men had to be carried to their corners – Sayers' right arm was useless. After two hours and twenty minutes, Heenan was virtually

19. *Above* Wrestlers, from the *Queen Mary Psalter*, c. 1310.

20. *Left* Wrestlers, from the *Luttrell Psalter*, c. 1340.

21. *Above* Tom Spring (left) and Bill Neate boxing at the Fives Court, drawn and engraved by I. R. Cruikshank in 1822 for *The Annals of Sporting and Fancy Gazette*, and published in 1825.

22. *Top right* Broughton v. Figg, published c. 1825. James Figg, Champion of boxing, the broadsword and the cudgel, discovered and trained John Broughton, and the two were the best-known fighters of their day.

blind from being continually hit in the eyes by Sayers' left: Sayers, for his part, was so weak that he could barely stand. At that juncture, Heenan took Sayers' head 'in chancery': the Umpires cut the ropes: the police broke in: the crowd surrounded the two boxers as, simultaneously, they knocked one another down. The result was declared to be a draw. It was a gory feat of bravery. For years afterwards, every American believed that Heenan was the winner: every Englishman that Sayers had won. It was not quite the last of the great bare-knuckle Championship fights, but it marked the beginning of their end.

Five years later, the Marquess of Queensberry introduced his 'Rules', which have substantially governed World boxing ever since. The amateurs of this age of 'Muscular Christianity' in English sport could accept this kind of boxing. The Queensberry – amateur – Championships, fought with gloves and at, originally, three controlled weights, began in 1867. The Amateur Boxing Association was formed in 1881 and the Public Schools felt able to embrace a sport now both manly and respectable. On the other – professional – side of the fence, bare-knuckle fights endured for some years but, by the early eighteen-nineties, gloves, limitation of rounds and matching by weights were accepted throughout the sport. Ironically enough, from the day that England produced the new Laws of Boxing, world dominance in it shifted to America.

Wrestling, though it had long found practitioners and spectators in London as well as the West, did not progress, as boxing did during the nineteenth century, into the realms of a major spectator sport. It continued to flourish in its ancient regional homes, in the South West and North West, where it remained fundamentally amateur: to be sure, winners might be given prizes, but the whole body of the sport was based on enthusiasm. So it was to continue into this century before other styles of wrestling were demanded in world competition.

THE CHASE

Hunting began, obviously enough, as a necessity. Animals were pursued for food or hunted down because they constituted a danger. Wolves roamed England in packs far into medieval times: the last of them were not stamped out until the beginning of the sixteenth century – much later in Scotland. The hunting of wolves and wild cats never captured the imagination; their destruction was a matter of social need and was carried out ruthlessly for the protection of human life and domestic stock.

The wild boar, however, was a different matter. It was an esteemed table delicacy and, unlike the wolf, it offered sport, with a spice of danger, for the huntsman. But although they endured much longer in Scotland and Ireland, the last recorded trace of a wild boar in England is 1683 – in Staffordshire – and it is doubtful if they had been hunted to any extent for some years before that date.

The most popular and least changed form of hunting in England for, probably, some two thousand years has been that of the hare. The reasons for this fact are good and have been consistently valid. The hare offers no danger; it makes good food; unlike the rabbit or the fox, it does not go to ground; it can be hunted from horseback or on foot and – perhaps best of all sporting reasons – it can be coursed by the greyhound, one of the oldest breeds of English dogs, one of great speed and grace, whose pursuit of the hare is a stirring sight. Indeed, it has given birth to a separate sport in coursing, which is, essentially, a competition between dogs which can be resolved without the catching or the death of the hare.

As late as the fourteenth century, however, it was an offence punishable with a year's imprisonment for any man who was not a property owner even to possess a greyhound – or any other dog or 'engine' which might take 'Gentlemen's games'.

In Roman and early Saxon times it was generally accepted that any man might take any wild creature on the unenclosed land which still comprised most of the country. Gradually, however, land was enclosed; and hunting became a royal sport.

The earliest of the great royal hunts were in pursuit of the stag. For almost a thousand years stag-hunting was the kingly sport of England. From Alfred and Canute through to Henry VII and James I, who was 'quite foolishly devoted' to the sport, English rulers hunted with elaborate ceremony. On some occasions the game was driven from cover through narrow passages in front of the royal stands to be killed virtually as 'sitting' targets. There is a record, too, of Queen Elizabeth I, before she came to the throne, hunting at Enfield, attended by twelve ladies-in-waiting, all dressed in white satin, a troop of archers in scarlet and one of yeomen in green. The cavalcade must have made a splendid sight but, lest it should appear impractical, it may be noted that, when a buck was brought down, the Princess herself cut its throat.

Otter-hunting, too, has a long history: for a considerable period the monarch was also 'Master of Otter Hounds' and James I compelled landowners in Norfolk to maintain packs of hounds for him. In earlier times the otter was hunted on foot: a servant would locate the otter's 'couch' in advance and the huntsmen would then attempt to spear the animal when it broke surface for air. Gradually otter-hounds were bred of a fine and sagacious quality and otter-hunting has remained a popular form of summer hunting in appropriate parts of England – notably the Fens.

Hawking – the hunting of other birds and game by the use of trained hawks – was established in Saxon England and continued in mounting favour until the introduction of fire-arms. Even after that it was cherished by a minority and constantly revived. There was an elaborate etiquette of hawk-

23. A Staffordshire pottery mug depicting Richard Humphreys (right) and Daniel Mendoza fighting at Odiham, in Hampshire, on 9th January, 1788. Humphreys chanced to see Mendoza engaged in a street fight and was impressed by his talent: as a result of his support and encouragement Mendoza gained a considerable reputation as a prize-fighter. They subsequently fell out, and fought against each other four times: Humphreys won the first two, Mendoza the third and fourth. This fight at Odiham was the second, won by Humphreys in 29 minutes.

ing: the type of bird a man might own depended upon his rank – from a gerfalcon for a king, and a falcon gentle for a prince, down through the falcon of the rock, a peregrine, bustard, sacre, laner, a merlyon (for a lady), a sparrow-hawk, a musket and a goshawk, to a tercel for a poor man. But that 'poor' man had to own property: the true poor were legally forbidden to own a hawk of any kind.

Different types of hawks were employed for different kinds of quarry: their training, whether they were reared from the nest or captured, was a long and highly skilful business and was the subject of some erudite books. The birds were beautiful and effective in action, rewarding to train and valuable as a property. Hawking was understandably a Royal enthusiasm which gave rise to a body of literature and art.

Oddly enough, the fox was the last quarry to become popular in England. That may seem surprising; but it is readily explicable. Until the middle of the eighteenth century the fox was barely considered worth the huntsman's attention. A gentleman might hunt for amusement but, if he wanted an element of danger, he pursued the wild boar; the otter afforded summer diversion; and it was pleasant to think that success in the chase would also benefit his kitchen in the shape of venison, boar or hare. The fox enjoyed only slight esteem for its fur and was regarded, simply enough, as vermin, as well destroyed, but not worth a gentleman's while to hunt for entertainment. Consequently they were usually trapped or shot as pests.

The change of attitude came after the Restoration, when further enclosures and much poaching during the Civil War had reduced the number of deer. There had been some fox-hunting earlier: Edward I kept foxhounds and there were packs in Yorkshire, Sussex and Leicestershire in the seventeenth century. But they were exceptions and not regarded as important.

A fair date for the beginning of the true fox-hunting tradition would be 1750. From that time onwards the sport grew until it became a part of English life, as revered on the one side as it was hated on the other. There has always been a

24. *Top Heading the Fox,* published in 1814 by C. Turner.

25. *Right Stag-hunting: Chopping at his head,* from *The Gentlemen's Recreation* by Richard Blome, published in 1686.

26. *Above* Frontispiece to the *Book of Falconrie,* 1498.

great bitterness – even if it could not always be declared – on the part of the tiller of the soil (often the tenant of a member of the hunt) towards those who hunt over his crops. Full-blooded fox-hunting cannot go side by side with good husbandry. Now began the line of legendary huntsmen – such men as Hugh Meynell, Squire Osbaldeston, Assheton Smith, John Mytton, Childe of Kinlet Hall (the first of the 'hard riders') and many more fearless Masters of the great Hunts. The strain of the foxhound was studied and improved. Horses were successfully bred for hunting. A literature grew up round the sport, through such writers as John Surtees, William Beckford, 'Nimrod' (C. J. Apperley) and the under-estimated Whyte-Melville. At only a slightly lower level than the best, too, there is a tradition of hunting art, produced by Leech and over a hundred years of artists who understood horses and hunting.

The traditional centre of fox-hunting is 'The Shires', roughly speaking Leicestershire, Northamptonshire and Rutlandshire though stretching beyond those counties, with such famous hunts as the Quorn, Cottesmore, Pytchley and Belvoir. About two hundred packs, though, are spread over England, all with their remembered great men, famous runs and cherished histories.

Often tenant farmers, local parsons or doctors rode with these packs. On the whole, however, the resources which enable a man to pay a hunt subscription, maintain a stable and find the free time to ride regularly to hounds are beyond all but the wealthy. Nevertheless the colour, life and excitement of the hunt still rouses many a non-huntsman to a cheer of enthusiasm as it passes, and many people still enjoy following the hounds on foot.

There is, too, one important qualification to be observed. If only the privileged may, nowadays, hunt the fox, many who do not share that privilege, including in some rare instances the farmers whose crops suffer from the hunt, have become imbued with the feeling – little short of a mystique – which the hunters themselves feel for it. Certainly some families have, for generation after generation, provided hunt servants in feudal fashion with complete enthusiasm. In some recent debates, fox-hunters have declared that the fox enjoys the hunt – and no fox has uttered a word of contradiction.

The social historian, without needing to mention foxes, hounds or horses, might argue that the most important effect of fox-hunting has been to produce a segment of society which has built its life round the hunt. Many men have devoted fortunes to running packs of hounds and have been more than content to hunt six days a week throughout the season. There probably are a hundred packs of hounds in the world outside Britain, most of them in the United States. But fox-hunting is essentially English and, in the eyes of many foreign nations, it is the typical – and often caricatured – English sport.

27. *The Southern Hounds, or Hunting in Its Infancy*, published in 1813 by C. Turner.

Hawker. In 1813 Hawker was invalided out of the Army. Several people challenged his claim to have invented the percussion cap, but there can be no doubt of his influence through the authorship of the classic of shooting, *Instruction to Young Sportsmen in All that Relates to Guns and Shooting*, which he published in 1814. That work was not merely constantly reprinted but remains in all the essentials the authoritative book on the subject. Hawker, a man of his time, used muzzle-loading guns: nevertheless, he was a superb marksman. More important, he laid down the enduring principles of what sporting England ever since has called, generically, 'shooting' which is to say largely partridge-shooting, pheasant-shooting, grouse-shooting and wild-fowling.

Grouse-shooting, which begins with some celebration on the Twelfth of August, is largely a North Country and even more a Scottish sport; though as many Englishmen as Scots shoot on the Scottish moors. Pheasant-shooting enjoyed its great period in the last quarter of the nineteenth century and the years to the first World War: it is in some ways an unnatural sport – the birds are driven from their homes and then turned back to provide difficult, fast, high-flying targets. Partridge-shooting was once the most general form of shooting practised all over the English countryside, particularly on small estates, but is now threatened by diminishing numbers of birds.

Wild-fowling is distinct from the other forms of shooting in that it is a sport of the wild places and not of the preserves and private estates. In some ways it calls for the highest of all shooting skills and for centuries it has been practised by the ordinary man as well as the guests of the great estates. It has evolved a richer lore and art than the other shooting sports enjoy.

The records of shooting in England include some 'bags' so enormous that one wonders the guns were not too hot to hold – or that any shoulder could stand the recoil of so many shots in a day. At the same time, Birmingham and London sporting guns established a standard unequalled by any others in the world.

28. *Hawking*, by Henry Alken, engraved by I. Clark. Plate 1 of *National Sports of Great Britain*, published in 1820.

Shooting – as a hunting sport, distinct from discharging the newly invented firearms for sheer excitement – dates from the first half of the nineteenth century. The early guns were perilous contraptions, often as dangerous to those who fired them as to the intended prey. Hand-guns existed in Italy by 1380: they were being commonly produced in Germany at the end of the fourteenth century and were imported into England in quantity for military purposes by Henry VII in 1486. By 1600 fowling pieces were commonly available in Britain but shooting as a measurable English sport begins with Colonel Peter

Fishing, like most forms of hunting, must also have begun for the pot. There is an odd excitement about netting or spearing fish but, far back beyond the beginning of print, there must have been a day when a man – or a boy – first experienced the excitement of 'tickling' a trout. Soon afterwards came the first man who, with rod and line – or simply a line – attempted to plumb and outwit the mind and reactions of the fish. Fishing always was, and still is, a mystery. When the bait is proffered to an invisible fish, a competition begins which has never been completely fathomed by man. Fishing is a sport at once profound, contemplative and impossible of complete understanding. Even in modern days of amazingly complicated equipment and aids, a man can go home with an empty bag. The choice of the fish to be caught, the planning of the place to fish, the type of equipment and the bait, the patience of the long wait, the exhilaration of the fish's 'take', the strike, the controlled skill of playing it and the ultimate landing of the catch, form a pattern of thought, composure, excitement and contentment which is a complete unity and a unique experience.

The ponds of the great monastic establishments of the Middle Ages were frequently so richly stocked – usually with trout – that fish for the table could be simply scooped out with the net. But there was extensive artificial – though sometimes accidental – stocking of lakes and rivers so that edible fish were plentiful and, for the angler, entertaining.

Izaak Walton, author of the much criticized but still widely accepted and richly evocative *The Compleat Angler*, understood the use of the wet fly; but the dry fly, most artful of lures – its creation so refined as to be a hobby in its own right, quite divorced from angling – was a nineteenth-century introduction.

Until the beginning of the industrial age, when salmon ran up the then unpolluted Thames and the Tyne and the other, now poisonous, rivers of England, a large proportion of the population could fish freely and with some hope of handsome and edible reward. To be sure, some salmon and trout fishing was private. One Victorian pundit, too, instructing on pike

fishing at its traditional best – in extremely cold weather – recommended that, in extreme temperatures, the gentleman angler should hand his rod to his man to lick the ice from the rings so that the line might run freely.

Gradually, as rivers became polluted and more people wanted to fish, more and more rivers were preserved in respect of game fishing – for salmon, trout and grayling. So,

29. A fox-hunting scene, by Thomas Rowlandson, 1787.

Of all the sports of the English, fishing is the most widely spread, through classes, age-groups, areas and periods. Hardly a town or village but is within fair distance of sea, river or lake: a rod can be elaborate and expensive for the man fishing his own salmon river: or as primitive as tree-branch, rigged with string and bent pin for the urchin dabbling hopefully in a turgid canal. Over the ages, men have reached a stage at which they can plan and wait for hours in acute discomfort to catch a fish, land it – probably weigh it – and then put it back into the water: this is true dedication to sport.

FOLK GAMES

The lack of early records and descriptions of sports and games is most apparent on the subject of early folk play. When Joseph Strutt wrote his *Sports and Pastimes of the People of*

3. PHEASANT SHOOTING

From a drawing by Samuel Howett, c. 1798. 17ins × 12ins

This is one of Samuel Howett's most characteristic pieces. He illustrated many sports, and drew an astonishing variety of animals, including elephants, tigers and otters, but his shooting scenes show his work at its best. His output was considerable; he was both designer and engraver, and since the colourists of his work are not usually named it is assumed that he also did most of this himself. Howett began drawing as an amateur, for enjoyment. He came from Chigwell, in Epping Forest, had independent means, and was free to indulge his inclinations towards field sports and careless good company. Money troubles drove him to professionalism, and he went to work as a drawing master at a Dr Goodenough's Academy in Ealing. Then, after a spell at Richmond in Yorkshire, he returned to the very centre of London, to Old Compton Street in Soho. Even after working for years in the city, he never lost his liking for the forests amongst which he grew up, and always drew them well, and with affection. He was described as 'wayward, congenial and vivacious'. He was a drinking companion of the artist George Morland, and married the sister of Thomas Rowlandson.

Having spent a fair part of his life following game with a long-barrelled fowling-piece, Howett knew the sport he was portraying, and his details are accurate. The dogs are near the men, so that they do not raise the birds out of range, 'slack mettled rather than hot-spirited', but they are ready to go when the bird drops, to find it in the thick undergrowth, and to bring it back uninjured in their soft spaniels' mouths. The huntsman is well caught in a stylish attitude that combines concentration and quickness of reaction.

during the nineteenth century, a distinction sharpened between game fishing and coarse fishing. It was crystallized, towards the end of that period, by J. W. Martin, 'The Trent Officer', who provided the major works of recollection and instruction for those growing numbers of anglers from the industrial towns of the north and the Midlands who fished frequently fouled rivers or canals for 'coarse' fish.

Angling clubs and competition fishing extended the scope of the angler, though hardly rapidly enough to keep pace with the increasing numbers who took up the hobby.

Sea-angling – with rod and line – followed automatically upon the expansion of the sport. It was a nineteenth-century development and the new 'pleasure piers' and the availability of hired boats on the coasts helped its growth, though it was to make its greatest advance in the present century.

30. *Trolling with the Gorge,* an 18th-century woodcut. Trolling is an angling technique still used today: a bright object – in this picture a piece of metal in the shape of a fish – is dragged through the water to attract surface-feeding fish.

Pheasant Shooting

England in 1801, many of the old games had disappeared, were limited to remote areas he did not know, or had been modified or amalgamated with others. So Strutt, at the end of his history, listed a number of 'Pastimes the Names of Which Are Not Known' and 'Amusements Mentioned by Various Writers and Not Described'.

We know that in England, as in almost all other civilizations, many dances survived the forgotten religions and rituals that first produced them. Their steps, rhythms and music were remembered, and performed seriously and responsibly, by the elders and passed on from generation to generation until relatively recent times. Those dances do not fall within our province here but they were probably as important as any of the holy day celebrations of medieval England.

There were, too, some dozens of games of varying kinds which can be identified. They vary from the completely primitive – like Hot Cockies in which one 'player' knelt with his eyes covered, while the others in turn buffeted him until he guessed who had struck a particular blow – to some slight degree of sophistication. There is little doubt that most, if not

all, these games were played in church buildings or churchyards. The church itself, or its cloisters, afforded a sheltered playing space, important in bad weather as the only building capable of accommodating the community. The church afforded the solid wall against which hand-ball, fives and kindred ball-sports grew up. Many games, too, needed a relatively smooth surface and this was often to be found, if not in a courtyard or cloister, in the churchyard. There a stretch of earth, usually on the north side of the church – 'the devil's side' in medieval superstition – would become a place of popular resort and was soon trodden flat by dancing and

31. *Top left Cat in a Bowl,* by Thomas Rowlandson, c.1780. Many of the popular games were basically cruel: some, such as the one pictured here, simply consisted of putting an animal in a painful or uncomfortable position and throwing stones at it.

32. *Above* The winter of 1813–14 was unusually severe, and at the beginning of February the Thames at London was completely frozen. A Frost Fair, with boxing booths, swings, skittles and side shows, was set up on the ice, and lasted three or four days.

33. *Top* Country sport c. 1785. One of the most popular of the traditional sports was 'catching the pig'. The pig's tail was soaped, and the object of the game was to catch hold of the tail and drag the pig backwards. It was not easy to do, and a success was followed by riotous celebrations.

34. *Above* The May Pole, c. 1824. Dancing round the May Pole on the first of May was a strong country tradition. Its origins were unknown, but it was well established by the middle of the 17th century.

35. *Right* A race held in the streets of the City of London, c. 1820.

games. In other cases there was a village green – usually adjoining the church – where the Maypole was set up.

The list of games is long and it includes many now regarded as childish, but which were played by the adults of an unlettered age – such as hop-scotch, various forms of 'tag', barley brake, 'touch last', 'base', 'hunt the fox', blind-man's-buff, leap-frog and the simpler ball games. It has been claimed that there is evidence for nine men's morris being played in Britain in the Stone Age, though most of the names for the game seem to derive from the Latin *merellus*, probably by way of the Norman-French *merelles*. Most easily described as a mixture of halma, draughts and noughts-and-crosses, nine men's morris could be played indoors on a board – many of which have survived to indicate its antiquity. It seems to have been played by people of all ages and classes in every part of England from at least the thirteenth century, and is still a pleasing diversion.

The churchyards certainly saw the growth, if not the origin, of the various games with marbles – like taw, boss out or nine holes – quoits, and the many forms of skittles and ninepins – such as kayles, cloish, loggats, Dutch pins. Apart from the ball games, and perhaps wrestling or boxing, these games called for little skill: they were essentially for an entire community, to amuse young and old and of both sexes; they were *play*, rather than competition – nearer to the singing, mumming and dancing that went with them than to modern sport.

It may be said, however, that there is hardly a children's game to be seen today which does not inherit something from the folk play of the Middle Ages, when people with little or no education or equipment devised them for their holy days' leisure.

BAITING

The concept of kindness – or at least of non-cruelty – to animals is relatively recent. In England only a few hundred years ago, cats were burnt in baskets as part of Guy Fawkes celebrations. Strutt records such 'amusements' as badger-baiting, in which a hole was dug in the ground for the animal and dogs were sent in one at a time to drag it out: duck-hunting – setting dogs after a duck on a pond: squirrel-chasing – by men in a house: rabbit-hunting – when rabbits were turned loose among a crowd of roisterous young men.

These were sports of merciless brutality towards relatively helpless animals. The better-known bull-baiting and bear-baiting, however, stemmed from different emotions. The lion, the wild cat, the wolf and the wild boar were gone: the dragon was recognized as a fiction. There remained, however, two animals which, in an age which did not know the tank, the armoured car, or the machine-gun, and which had forgotten the fighting chariot, were terrifying in their power. They were the bear and the bull. Both were baited – usually tethered – and worried by dogs, in special 'rings' with ample spectator accommodation. The dogs suffered, of course, and were often killed. Bulls and bears, however, were too costly to be killed, and the baiting ended when the dogs were routed or the bigger animal was in distress – leaving its owner-keeper (or the ward employed by the local council) to patch it up as quickly as possible for the next 'entertainment'.

The famous bear-garden at Southwark was once owned by

James I and there were permanent bull rings in many towns. The infamous running of a bull through the streets of Stamford to its eventual killing continued, despite the use of troops in an attempt to stop it, until 1840: and it is said that there was a bull-baiting near Liverpool as recently as 1853. Thus the Englishman for centuries up to 150 years ago lulled his fear of these mighty animals.

Cock-fighting had a certain following such as the other anti-animal sports never possessed. Specially bred gamecocks, often with sharp metal sheaths fitted to their spurs, were trained to fight and did so in a manner which moved some effective writers and artists to record their battles. Cock-fighting drew appreciable crowds, and betting on it was often extremely heavy.

James I was an enthusiast for cock-fighting, bear-baiting and bull-baiting, and he once attempted to bait the lions kept in the Tower of London.

Except in a few isolated instances, the sports which involved baiting with dogs did not survive the legislation of the early nineteenth century. Cock-fighting, however, had many supporters, some of them powerful, such as Admiral Rous who protested against its suppression even as late as 1875.

Cock-fighting, in fact, persisted long after public cockpits were declared illegal – in 1849 – and it is reported that the devotees of the sport may still, occasionally, be advised of a 'main' to be fought, in secret, in the North Country. Dog-fights – between dogs carefully bred for the purpose – and ratting, too, continued long after baiting was suppressed.

In general, however, the more blatantly cruel sports involving death or damage to animals have been shamed out of existence – though, of course, foxes, otters, deer, stags, grouse, partridges, pheasants, hare, wild fowl and rabbits are still killed for sport.

36. *Top left* Bull against dogs, by Theodore Lane, from *Anecdotes of the Turf, the Chase, the Ring and the Stage* by Pierce Egan, 1827. Bull-baiting never became as popular in England as bear-baiting, although it gave rise to the breed of dogs known as 'bull-dogs'.

37. *Above* Bear-baiting, published in 1825. A match held at Combe Warren in 1824 for dogs against a champion bear: the prize was a silver collar.

HORSE SPORTS

The matching of horses must date from the first days when men rode, and we know that the Romans raced horses and chariots in Britain. For many years English horses – employed to drag ploughs, sleighs and carts through mud or to carry knights clad in weighty armour – tended towards plodding thickness rather than speed. Speed, however, is a relative matter: a race between two carthorses is a race: and gradually some strains fined down, gained speed and a long stride.

Through the Middle Ages most horse races were either the contest of two men's horses for a wager, or to exhibit the paces of horses which were for sale – as we know happened in the twelfth century when there was a horse-market at Smithfield. About that time, too, there are records of some racing in Easter and Whitsun festivals. The first concrete evidence of an organized race meeting is of one held on the Roodee at Chester in 1539. At first the winner was given a wooden ball, of some now unremembered significance, but later it was altered to a silver bell – which became so much a traditional award that the important early race courses were called 'bell courses' and to 'bear the bell away' passed into common parlance as a term for one pre-eminent in any walk of life.

Gradually the sport took root during the Tudor period, as a hobby of royalty and the nobility. Henry VIII employed a trainer and jockeys: and horse races were often included in the displays organized for his, or Queen Elizabeth's, royal visits. But it first became truly 'The Sport of Kings' – in the reign of James I, who not only gave it immense impetus by his presence and support at Newmarket, but also took the historic step of importing the famous 'Markham Arabian', the first major move in English bloodstock breeding.

Cromwell suppressed horse-racing but, with the Restoration, Charles II made Newmarket one of his social centres, rode and backed his own horses there, and confirmed it as the hub of racing in England.

William III, a keen gambler on horses – and a notoriously irascible loser – continued to import bloodstock and, under his patronage, the number of races and courses increased until, by 1727, there were more than a hundred race meetings a year in England.

Riding schools, too, began to spring up: the momentum increased. Queen Anne, an enthusiast for the hunt, encouraged

38. *Above* Stag-hunting, from a 14th-century manuscript.

39. *Right* Jousting, from a 14th-century manuscript.

races for hunters, in particular at Ascot, in an attempt to improve the strain. Her reign saw the acquisition of the Darley Arabian, one of the great stallions which established the quality of English race-horses. Over the preceding 300 years since the time of Richard II, several types of English horses had shed the former ponderous quality. Now their natural long stride was linked with the stamina and fire of the Arab to produce the magnificent strain which has held its place in the subsequent history of racing throughout the world.

The second half of the eighteenth century saw racing set on a firm footing. The Jockey Club was formed – at that celebrated resort of fashionable sportsmen, The Star and Garter coffee-house – in about 1750 and, as its influence spread out beyond Newmarket, it ensured that there was some degree of organization in racing. In 1765 the greatest of race-horses – the never beaten Eclipse – was foaled in the stables of the Duke of Cumberland, third son of George III. Fifteen years later, the first Derby was run at Epsom, and was won by Sir Charles Bunbury's Diomed, second only to Eclipse among the great English sires. In 1778 the first St Leger stakes was run on the Doncaster Corporation's new course.

By now horse-racing was a popular sport with all classes –

though on the course the barriers between them remained insurmountable. Kings attended the major meetings and so did the poorest – as hawkers, stable-boys, servants, or simply beggars. But Epsom Downs, Newmarket, Ascot and Doncaster were places of general and gay resort during their great meetings.

Unhappily but naturally, wagering made the sport corrupt. The Act restricting winnings or losses on a horse race to £10 had been treated with contempt for many years before its repeal at the time of the creation of the Jockey Club. Heavy betting has always bred dishonesty, and nowhere more violently than in horse-racing.

The comments, by a German observer (Puckler-Muskau) that 'cheating in every kind of sport was common in England' and by the Frenchman (Misson) about aristocratic English

40. *Left* Trotting never achieved the popularity in England that it gained in America, but for a short while in the early 19th century it enjoyed some support. This portrait of a trotter is by J. F. Herring (1795–1865).

41. *Above* A horse-match at Newmarket between Grey Wyndham, a horse belonging to his Grace the Duke of Somerset, and Bay Bolton. Grey Wyndham is winning comfortably: the old man in the right foreground has apparently forgotten, in his excitement, to beat his drum to celebrate the victory. By John Wootton (1678?–1765), engraved by Roger Rooe.

race-goers that it was 'common for them to lay wagers of two thousand guineas on a single race' were the result of objective observation. Bribery, pulling, substitution of horses and appalling trickery were prevalent. Tregonwell Frampton, later called 'The Dictator of the Turf', having wagered that he could produce the fastest gelding in the country, castrated Dragon, the finest horse in Britain, and put him into the race, which the Dragon won before he died, in agony, from the operation.

The Jockey Club was powerful, but not *all*-powerful. It 'warned off' the Prince Regent – later George IV – but, when there were grounds for believing in dishonesty at such a level, the problem was not easily to be solved.

In 1812 Danny Dawson, a hanger-on of horse-racing, was hanged at Cambridge for poisoning horses by putting arsenic in their troughs at Newmarket – and it was said that the instigator of his crime kept him quiet at the crucial time by assuring him that he would be reprieved. Lord George Bentinck – an idealist in every way, and an enthusiastic owner who evinced great consideration for his horses – had the most powerful corrective effect on racing. As late as 1844, a four-year-old and a five-year-old were run in the Derby under false names: one of them fell while in the lead and the other 'won'. Bentinck challenged the 'result' in the courts and won his case. Tattersalls introduced and maintained a high level of integrity in horse-sales and control of betting. But, though many honest men worked to 'clean up' racing, they achieved only partial success. Yet if it was not virtuous, it was colourful. Frith's well known painting, 'Derby Day', reveals how complete a cross-section of the Victorian public swarmed to the races on Epsom Downs, creating an extent of human warmth and response such as no other English sport had yet known.

The nineteenth century, with its gift for creating 'stars', threw up Fred Archer – 'The Flying Tinman' – one of the greatest of all jockeys. Archer was a cruel rider but his ability was beyond doubt and, in 1880, he established himself in the hearts of the Victorian public when, with one arm all but

42. *Above* Derby Day, 27th May, 1871. It was known as 'The Baron's Year', because Baron Meyer de Rothschild won four of the five 'classic' races, as the Oaks, the St. Leger, the 1000 and 2000 guineas and the Derby were called. His horse, Favonius, overtook Digby halfway up the straight, and won comfortably by 1½ lengths. Albert Victor and King of the Forest dead-heated for second place.

43. *Right Coming In* – the Hunters Stakes, run on Port Meadow, near Oxford, on August 4th, 1802. Drawn and engraved by Charles Turner. The horses were drawn in by J. L. Agasse, for which commission he was paid five guineas by Turner.

useless from an earlier accident, he came through from far behind to win the Derby by a head on Bend Or. It might not be pure, but it was heroic, and that section of the English public which did not regard racing as sin loved it. On the cold basis of economics, of course, horse-racing had long been important in terms of employment, the sale and export of bloodstock and all the by-products of a major entertainment industry.

Steeplechasing, which began as races between huntsmen across country with a distant steeple as their objective, originated in Ireland, and was enthusiastically taken up in The Shires towards the end of the eighteenth century. Briefly it flourished in London, at 'The Hippodrome' which stood where Ladbroke Square now is. Since then it has divided sharply in two different directions. Point-to-point races are still considerable country events, especially in the fox-hunting districts, where this is still a sport for huntsmen and their horses. On the other side, since the formation of the Grand National Hunt Committee in 1866, National Hunt racing, with its peak the Grand National, run at Aintree, has become the winter aspect of horse-racing.

Polo, launched by the officers of the 10th Hussars in 1869 on the basis of the Indian 'hockey on horseback' has, ever since, retained an enthusiastic minority following, largely military, and with sharp class barriers.

Coaching as a sport grew up and died within the nineteenth century. Wealthy men engaged, and wagered on, the famous professional coachmen of the day or, preferably, bought coaches, strove to master the difficult skills required to drive a coach-and-four, and raced against one another. Between 1807 and 1870, such famous coaching clubs as the Bessington, the Four-Horse, the Richmond, the Four-in-Hand and, finally, the Coaching Club, were formed. The hobby faded with the decline in coaches and disappeared in face of the introduction of the motor car.

The records of sport, for obvious reasons, contain no mention of the vast number of people who, over the ages, have derived infinite pleasure simply from riding a horse, without

thought of competition. Though there are today competitions in horsemanship at Olympic level, riding for centuries has been delight. To the young, merely to be on horseback, was, and still is, an immense childish excitement; in all classes, riding has been an uncomplicated pleasure.

WATER SPORTS

Sport on the water is a comparatively recent idea among the English. Until the late eighteenth century they thought nothing of the seaside as a place of pleasure. Swimming might

44. Boat Race on the River Isis at Oxford, by I. T. Serres, engraved by John Whessell, 1822. The Universities took to rowing around the beginning of the 19th century, but the sport did not take on organized form until the 1820s, when 'bumping' races were invented on rivers, such as the Isis, which were too narrow for boats to line up abreast. The boats proceeded down the river in line, and by bumping the boat in front the crew gained the right to exchange places with it in the following heat.

be useful as a military qualification for soldiers or sailors; sailing and rowing were essential facets of transport and trade. But after the Romans – who esteemed baths more than anyone in England was to do for many centuries after they left – swimming was not popular and, in fact, it was forbidden, on pain of severe punishment, to students at Cambridge in Elizabethan times.

Children, and often their elders, plunged into cool rivers and streams in warm weather: but that was an altogether different matter from developing the mechanics of swimming.

Some people who lived by the water learnt to swim as an insurance but the first indication we have of swimming enjoying any public esteem is at the time of the Restoration, when rowing and yachting also showed signs of becoming popular. In 1734 there was an open-air swimming pool in London, near the present Old Street Station and, as the century developed, 'dipping' in the sea became one of the attractions of the new 'seaside resorts'.

Here, as elsewhere, the nineteenth century provided patronage, administration and a major figure. The spread of public baths – primarily for reasons of hygiene – led many people to learn to swim. At Eton, everyone who rowed had to be able to swim and with, as usual, public schoolboys in the forefront, an organizing body – the Amateur Swimming Association – was set up in 1886.

The sharpest spur to the public imagination was the amazing feat of a Captain Webb from Dawley, who, in 1875, swam from Dover to Calais – the first man to swim across the Channel without artificial aids. His feat was the talk of England and it fired many with enthusiasm.

Water polo developed from the boom in swimming. During the 1870s, under the name of Aquatic Football, it evolved spontaneously in a number of different places and in different forms, played with anything from a tennis ball to a football, between teams of from three to fifteen in number, and with goals and pitches of all sizes. By the 1880s, though, a uniform code of Laws had been formulated: a League followed and, within a decade, water polo was an international sport.

45. *Above* Gosport Regatta, by John Harris, c.1811. Dedicated to Dr. H. Burney and the pupils of the Royal Academy, Gosport, Hants.

46. *Right* Sea bathing, 1814.

Rowing, like any other test of speed, would have happened spontaneously. But, except in the Navy, we hear of little competitive rowing until the eighteenth century. It was in 1715 that a comedian named Thomas Dogget first put up the 'Coat and Badge' by which his name is still remembered for a race between watermen on the Thames.

Here, again, the sport fell into the familiar Victorian mould. It was taken up by Eton, Westminster, Amateur clubs in the London area, Oxford and Cambridge Universities (with bumping races between college crews on the Isis and the Cam). In 1829 the first University Boat Race – at Henley – was won by Oxford. The second did not take place until 1836 and it did not become a regular annual event until 1856. It was transferred to London, first to a course between Westminster and Putney and then, as river traffic grew more dense, to the now familiar Putney-to-Mortlake. To general surprise – for rowing has always been a minority sport in England and was especially so in the Victorian period – the event drew huge crowds from the start and soon was one of the most popular of all English sporting events, followed in passionately partisan fashion by thousands of people with no connections whatever with either University. Boat building made great strides to produce craft and oars for eights, fours, pairs and single sculls; and technique, too, improved rapidly.

Regattas – arranged, at first, with some hesitation – became highly successful. The greatest was, and still is, Henley, which even before 1900 attracted major overseas crews. But there were a large number of others, especially on the Thames, though also on rivers and estuaries around England.

The historians of sailing as a sport are usually content to credit its introduction to Charles II – that relisher of so many pleasures – who took delight in sailing a twenty-ton craft presented to him by the East India company. In 1662, Charles sailed and won a race from Greenwich to Gravesend against the Duke of York. Little of note seems to have happened for about another hundred years when there was a fashion for small boat sailing on the Thames though this, again, was a pursuit of relatively wealthy people. The Royal Thames Yacht

Club was formed in 1775 and there was a sailing race round the Isle of Wight in 1788. But it was not until 1815 that some 'people of condition' formed the Royal Yacht Club, later the Royal Yacht Squadron. Other clubs, most of them under Royal patronage, sprang up round the coast and during the nineteenth century Cowes Week became one of the most exclusive sporting and social occasions of the calendar. As it grew in eminence it also grew further away from the common people, who could not join in for lack of craft, and could not watch it adequately because so much of it took place out of their sight that they simply could not understand what was going on. The Squadron's own historian in 1903 described yachting at Cowes as 'a sport of millionaires'. So it remained until well into the present century before ordinary people

47. Hull Grand Regatta, July 31st, 1851, by W. F. Settle, engraved by T. G. Sutton. The cutter yacht, Kingston (left), is pictured crossing the finishing line to win the Challenge Cup.

48. *Top* Draughts, from a 14th-century manuscript.

49. *Above* Chess, from a 15th-century manuscript.

could buy – and find the leisure to sail – small boats of their own.

If skating may be said to fall into the category of water sports, it affords an altogether different picture. Englishmen from the earliest times have slid or skated whenever their lakes, ponds and rivers have frozen. At first they improvised skates from the bones of animals – ox or horse – but, by the time of the Restoration, Dutch iron-bladed models were often to be found in England. The first skating club in history was formed in Edinburgh in 1742 and the first in London exactly a century later.

ATHLETICS

The simplest of all forms of non-violent competition between human beings is that of trying to move from one point to another faster, or to jump farther than an opponent. Next might well come the attempt to throw a rock, a stick or a spear, farther than another man. Those are the constant ingredients of athletics.

There can be no question that, through all history – in England as elsewhere – human beings, from childhood onwards, have reacted to these challenges. For centuries the English ran, leapt and threw for fun at their feats and games. An impromptu race could be started, run, won and forgotten in minutes. In some cases it seems possible that foot-races had a religious significance. In parts of Derbyshire and Yorkshire the custom of young men racing in the nude 'for the bride's garter' persisted into the nineteenth century. In general, however, it seems that men raced for the exhilaration of matching their speed against another's.

For hundreds of years the Cornish Games and the Cotswolds Games, which annually drew huge crowds, included athletics prominently in their programmes, and Henry VIII was said to excel at 'Casting the barre' (throwing the hammer).

It was simply a reflection of social life that in the seventeenth century foot races began to assume popular importance. Noblemen employed footmen – not what the present day understands as footmen, but men employed to deliver messages on foot and with the greatest possible speed. Thus they became, almost by accident, trained runners, constantly in practice, learning to control their stride, adjust their pace to the distance they had to go, and to husband their strength. What more natural in a gambling society than that their masters should match, and back, their men in races? So, as early as the 1660s, Pepys could refer to footraces in Hyde Park and on Banstead Downs attracting attention among Londoners.

In the next century, more and more wealthy men employed and trained fast runners as footmen, and there was much and heavy wagering on their races. Many of the races were freakish: thus men might run under the handicap of loads, or with 'jockeys' on their backs. In 1788, huge crowds came to Newmarket Heath to watch a runner named Evans make good his claim that he could run ten miles in an hour.

Athletics made its first profound impact in the early days of the nineteenth century and, as so often then, one person caught the imagination. A certain Captain Barclay – hailed as

4. ROYAL NORTHERN YACHT CLUB

From a print dedicated to His Grace the Duke of Portland (Commodore), the Vice Commodore and Members of the Club, engraved by E. Duncan from the painting by W. Clark of Greenock, and published by Alex M. Findlay. 23ins × 15½ins

The Royal Northern Yacht Club was founded in 1824, by 'certain gentlemen in the North of Ireland and the West of Scotland addicted to the sport of yachting'. The club had two bases, one at Rothesay on the Clyde, the other in Belfast Lough. The flag of the Scottish section was a lion rampant surrounded by thistles, and of the Irish shamrocks surrounding a harp. The Northern Irish branch was dissolved in 1838, and in 1866 the Royal Ulster Yacht Club was formed to replace it.

The regatta in the picture probably took place about 1840. The Club – as one can see by the guests and ladies aboard the Commodore's boat – had a flourishing social life. The full dress uniform of the members was a blue coat lined with red silk, white or black pantaloons or breeches, and silk stockings of a corresponding colour, and members who appeared at the club's dinners 'improperly dressed' were fined ten shillings. Edward Duncan, who engraved this print, was a water colour painter who specialised in coastal scenery and shipping, and learned his aquatinting during his apprenticeship to the London engraver Robert Howell. He was highly thought of as an etcher and lithographer, and did some fine work in collaboration with the painter William John Huggins.

This Plate is respectfully Dedicated to His Grace The Duke of Portland, (COMMODORE), The Vice Commodore, and Members of the ROYAL NORTHERN YACHT CLUB, By their most Obedient Servant, ALEX. M. FINDLAY.

an expert in 'pedestrianism' – undertook to walk a thousand miles in a thousand hours, and did so. Barclay – his real name was Barclay Allardice – became a public hero: a book was written about him and the young bloods who had reacted to all the sporting fashions, from fencing to boxing, now turned to running and walking.

The rural games went on, where men chased pigs, ran blindfold or in three-legged races. But now there was a parallel stream which was already quite serious and soon was to produce 'modern' athletics. The most significant early event was probably the athletics meetings arranged at the Royal Military College at Sandhurst in 1810. By the middle of the nineteenth century there were athletics clubs at Oxford and Cambridge and in 1865 they held the first University running match. Clubs were now being formed all over the country and in 1880, in the typical Victorian mould, the Amateur Athletic Association was formed to administer the sport.

It might be argued that the significant date of the change in the main character of athletics was 1884 when an Englishman, W. L. George, set the first accepted record for the mile – the race which had already captured the English imagination – at 4 minutes 18.4 seconds.

Again the public schools fell into strongly supporting line and athletics took immense strides forward to the 1890s. In 1896 England competed in the revival of the Olympic Games, at Athens: and, in the 1900 Games at Paris, British runners won the 800 and 1500 metres events.

By 1900 the day of specialization in sport was dawning and the period of the great all-rounder was waning. The nineteenth century in England produced some of the most versatile sportsmen the world has ever known. 'Squire' Osbaldeston was a master of foxhounds, a magnificent horseman, cricketer, shot, runner, oarsman and tennis player. His contemporary and rival Thomas Assheton Smith, similarly Master of the Quorn Hunt, was probably a better boxer but not Osbaldeston's match at cricket and barely his equal at shooting. The Hon. Alfred Lyttelton played for England at cricket and football, was an outstanding tennis player and represented his University at both athletics and rackets. C. B. Fry was also an international cricketer and footballer, ran the 100 yards for Oxford and held the world record for the long jump for twenty-one years. These men were the last flowering of the gifted ones who played many games brilliantly and simply for fun.

BALL GAMES

Ball games are the outstanding form of English play for two important reasons. They, earlier and more definitely than any other kind of sport, bridged the social gap and, secondly, they demand an aptitude – usually termed ball-sense – which of old, if not nowadays, seemed more common among the British than most other races.

There have been many forms of activity with the ball in English life – some of them recalled but not known by an exact name, others named, but not described. They altered in form and status over the centuries until they fell into seven distinct groups, characterized by football, tennis, bowls, croquet, cricket, hockey and golf.

50. *Left* A six-day pedestrian race held at the Agricultural Hall, Islington, in 1870.

51. *Top* A pedestrian hobbyhorse, published in 1819. One of the many predecessors of the bicycle, the hobbyhorse was propelled by sitting on the saddle and running. Unhappily it never enjoyed any popular success.

52. *Above* The London gymnasium, c. 1821. In the early 19th century there was a revival of athletics, probably as a result of the growth of English public schools. The interest created spread to Universities, and eventually created a demand for organized events.

Football is an ancient game. The original ball was, according to some legends, the head of a Danish invader killed in battle: in other instances, as at Chester where a painted wooden ball was used, the game seems likely to have derived from some pagan ritual. In the many districts where football was traditionally played at Shrovetide it probably perpetuated some ancient local rivalry.

In the earlier games the 'ball' varied in size, shape and construction: the goals, small or large, might be several miles apart: the 'pitch' might be streets, open country or both: and a 'team' sometimes contained almost every able-bodied man in a district. The ancient matches had an evil reputation for violence and, in consequence, they were widely condemned and in many cases forbidden. So Strutt, in 1801, could write 'Foot ball was formerly much in vogue among the common people of England, though of late years it seems to have fallen into disrepute, and is but little practised'. Yet even as he wrote, the game was being played enthusiastically in – of course – the public schools. At Charterhouse and Westminster it was played in the cloisters; at Rugby and Cheltenham, over wide areas of open field, while Eton, Winchester, Harrow and Shrewsbury all had their own particular variants. In 1823 at Rugby School, according to the plaque there, 'William Webb Ellis, with a fine disregard for the rules of football as played in his time, first took the ball in his arms and ran with it, thus originating the distinctive feature of the Rugby Game.'

At Cambridge, in 1846, a code of rules was framed which sought to reconcile all the different forms of the game and it provided a satisfactory basis for play at the University for some years. Meanwhile, football had been introduced in the North. Sheffield – the oldest football club in the world – was formed in 1855 and, all at once, the game spread throughout the country. The old boys of the public schools were generally the more accomplished players, but the working men's and church clubs grew rapidly in numbers and ability.

In 1863, representatives of the public schools, the Universities and leading clubs met in London to draw up a code of laws. Their first four meetings seemed to lead towards agree-

53. *Above* Billiards, by H. Bunbury, c. 1790.

54. *Right* A game of croquet in 1870, when it was at its peak of popularity as a fashionable garden-party game. Croquet was brought to England from France in about 1860.

ment: the fifth ended in failure and in the definite split between the two codes – Association and Rugby – which was to grow even wider with the years. The major dispute at the time was whether to allow hacking and tripping – as the Rugby group wished – or not: oddly enough, running with the ball in the hands was a lesser issue.

From that date, although they continued for a few years

under an uneasy common administration, there were two forms of football. The distinction has been defined thus – 'One is a gentlemen's game played by hooligans, and the other a hooligan's game played by gentlemen'. Both spread throughout Britain on all levels of society and eventually – though in this respect the Association game was more successful than Rugby – across the world.

Just as football had split into two codes, so soccer divided into two sections. The professional game could only exist as a spectator sport, financed out of gate receipts. In this respect it was a product of the new Saturday half-day and the workers of the great industrial areas embraced it with demanding warmth.

The amateur game was, and is, a game for players: there belong not only the old boys' clubs but the services and village teams who play, on differing planes of ability, simply for pleasure – and who outnumber the professionals by hundreds to one.

The football of the professional clubs has had a deep effect not only on its players, but on its spectators. When, in the 1880s and 1890s, the teams from Blackburn, Birmingham, Liverpool, London, Nottingham, Wolverhampton, Derby, Sheffield and Bury came to play in the Cup Final at Kennington Oval or Crystal Palace, they were followed by crowds of supporters. Cup Final Day became the occasion of an annual invasion of the capital by what a reporter called 'the cloth-capped hordes'. It was the first mass encounter between the working men of London and those of the industrial provinces: it remains a salutary experience on both sides.

Rugby did not spread quite so quickly, nor so strongly, except in Wales and the London suburbs. But its development was more democratic. Until the Rugby League breakaway of 1895 on the issue of 'broken time' payments to players, it was an all-amateur sport. It consciously rejected the idea of leagues or cup competitions which might encourage professionalism and, over the years, by trial and error, clubs worked out fixture lists compatible with their playing strength. The major occasions of the domestic season were, and still are, the

University Match and international games between the Home countries. Socially, Rugby has always included a generous cross section of the community, from the Universities to the pits and iron foundries and, by comparison with soccer, it has been singularly free from corruption and local self-interest.

By the end of the nineteenth century, goalposts of one type or the other – or both – stood in every village in England: in the larger towns, the gaunt, iron grandstands were being mellowed by the weather into established parts of the landscape, and on Saturday afternoons they rattled with cheers which rang in the ears of people whole streets away.

The games of the group which includes 'real' tennis, lawn tennis, fives, rackets, squash rackets and handball were, until 1900 – and still are in essence – for players rather than spectators. They spring purely from the country churchyards and the cloisters.

The basic game was simply 'handball', which consisted of one player hitting a ball with his hand against the church wall and his opponent returning the rebound, and so on, until one failed to make the return. The refinements of fives derive from the architectural details of the church: where there was a buttress, the ball might be bounced off it on to the 'front wall'. An offset plinth – two-feet-six from the ground at Rugby, four-feet-six at Eton – dictated the height on the front wall for

55. *Left* A detail from a 16th-century painting depicting the story of David and Bathsheba. It is one of the earliest known representations of tennis.

56. *Top* Ball game, from the *Luttrell Psalter*, c. 1340.

57. *Above* Trap ball, 14th century.

47

58. *Top* Football at the Wall, from *A Few Recollections of Eton*, published in 1840. The traditional Wall Game played at Eton College is extremely complicated, and bears little resemblance to either soccer or Rugby football.

59. *Above* Tennis, from *Orbis Sensualium Pictus* by John Amos Comenius, 1659.

the return which was 'up'; while the Eton and Winchester forms of the game were clearly dictated by the architecture there – the step and 'pepper box' in one case, the semi-buttress in the second. At times there were complaints from the clergy about the noisy thump of fives balls against the wall and sometimes, too, windows were broken. So, in a number of churchyards in south Somerset, one may still see the separate walls built away from the church for the use of the fives players.

An important form of the game is often ignored – the simple, basic handball, still played against the blank walls of houses or factories by working men in north east England on quite as high a level of skill as may be found in the recognized forms of fives.

The original handball was played bare-handed but, in the course of time, some of the players sought to protect their hands and increase the power of their hitting by wearing gloves – as fives players still do. Some put stuffing in the gloves: the next step was to hold a piece of board in the hand – and, eventually, a racket.

The sport of rackets – similar to fives but played with a racket – has a peculiar history. It was evolved in English jails, notably the debtors' prison, the Fleet. In 1820, Robert Mackay, a debtor of unsavoury reputation, became the first accepted champion of a sport which, like so many others, was quickly adopted by the public schools. When Sir William Hart Dyke, a Harrovian, won the Championship in 1862, he was said to be the first holder of the title who had not learnt the game in prison.

Squash rackets, played with a soft ball and in a smaller court, began as an offshoot of rackets and was also adopted by the public schools. It grew quickly in popularity though, as with fives and rackets, its extent is limited by the number of courts.

The 'classic' form of court games is tennis – called 'royal' or 'real' or 'court' tennis to distinguish it from lawn tennis. One of the earliest of all ball games and probably originally French, it seems to have remained largely unaltered for about a thousand years. The oldest ball game court in the world is the tennis court that Henry VIII had built at Windsor Castle in 1529. Large and elaborate, with penthouse and a sloping roof over the galleries, dedans and grille – which were no doubt originally based on some particular cloister – a tennis court is almost prohibitively expensive, though some of Henry VIII's nobles constructed them for his visits. The game is involved, and calls for considerable skill, strength and stamina. Though it was once forbidden to the lower orders, it has never been truly popular, if only for lack of courts. Latterly, centred on the court at Lord's Cricket Ground, it has reached an extremely high point of skill both among amateurs and the professionals who are employed as coaches.

Lawn tennis, the latest of this group of games to achieve widespread popularity, has become one of the two truly world-wide sports. Its history in England is mixed. Obviously, children played it over the churchyard wall or hedge, so that Chaucer wrote simply of 'playen racket to and fro': and

48

COURSING, A VIEW IN HATFIELD PARK

towards the end of the eighteenth century it was widely popular under the name of 'field tennis'.

For a number of reasons – particularly the advance of cricket – lawn tennis languished for a considerable part of the nineteenth century. Then, in 1874, Major Wingfield applied for a patent for his 'invention' which he called 'Sphairistike' – 'a new and improved portable court for playing the ancient game of tennis'. From that time lawn tennis improved and spread at an amazing rate. For many it was a vicarage lawn amusement, a gentle, even genteel, kind of pat-ball. In its other sector, its techniques were being explored and exploited so quickly that it became a sport of major importance not merely in England but, at a step, throughout the world. It is possible, however, that the most historically significant facet of Victorian lawn tennis is that, first in Maud Watson and then in the mighty Lottie Dod, it ushered women into sporting competition at the highest level.

Bowls is another of the obvious games. Clearly, the elderly and less active males 'invented' it independently as their game at village feasts. It does not seem to have received any enduring record until, in 1541, Puritan objections to the extent of betting on it produced a law which forbade the keeping of a bowling alley for profit. But for centuries the rolling of a ball – at a 'jack', a single pin, ninepins or skittles – had been a popular game in town and country. The law endured, and was generally ignored, until 1845. In the meantime, greens were laid in private estates of the gentry and in the gardens of taverns, and in many towns the bowling-green became the place of popular – even civic – resort. James I had played the game – while forbidding it to the common people – but he could not suppress it: bowls is a natural game.

Golf was an importation from Scotland. The Roman Paganica is said to have been similar; bandy was something of a cross between golf and hockey, while pall mall – which won royal favour in the seventeenth century – was a mixture of golf and croquet. But golf was an established Scottish game when James I and his courtiers introduced it to England. It sent down isolated roots at Blackheath and Westward Ho! but

made no appreciable impact on the English during the two and a half centuries before Edward VII – while still Prince of Wales – made it fashionable in the latter part of the Victorian period, and its real rise did not come until the present century.

Hockey, under a wide range of regional names, was played in England from the sixteenth century. It may have incorporated some ingredients from the Irish hurling, bandy and some Scottish games, while a traditional Shrove Tuesday play of similar method on the sands at Scarborough was undoubtedly ancient in origin. Hockey was given final definition, and the Hockey Association was formed, in 1886 and, as a player sport

60. *Football played at the Market Place, Barnet*, drawn and engraved by Bowles and Carver, c. 1740. A typical example of the rough-and-tumble football which was played at fairs or on special holidays. On occasions forty or fifty players would join in, and the riots which inevitably followed caused the game to be banned until the beginning of the 19th century.

of both men and women, it took firm root in the next dozen years.

At one point in the nineteenth century, croquet, which derived from several other games, reached great heights of popularity as a genteel, but not aristocratic game which might be played by both sexes despite the long skirts and tight corsets of the age. It was soon to be relegated to complete unimportance but briefly it was embraced, with chaste enthusiasm, by the Victorian middle class.

Cricket provides the strongest survivor and, in a way, the amalgamation, of a number of early games such as cat-and-dog and knur-and-spell – in both of which a billet of wood, and not a ball, was struck with a bat or stick – stoolball, which still flourishes as a game, largely of women, in Sussex – club ball and bat-and-trap. Cricket included the elements of three primitive forms of play: in the first, a man aimed a ball at a target; in the second, his opponent defended the target against the ball with a club, and, thirdly, he attempted to strike the ball away.

The simple lack of smooth and level ground which confined so many medieval sports to the churchyard must have limited early cricket to the close downland turf or land grazed by sheep. Therefore it was born in the Weald and grew up in the counties of Kent, Sussex, Hampshire and Surrey. By little more than the accident of an archivist's discovery, the record was unearthed of a certain John Derrick deposing, in 1598, that fifty years earlier, when he was a pupil there, cricket was played at the Guildford Free School.

It can be tenably argued that cricket began when one shepherd boy rolled a ball of twisted wool at the gate of a sheepfold while his fellow attempted to strike it away with his crook. It is certain, however, that the game was strongly established by midway through the eighteenth century, when it had a clearly defined, and printed, code of laws. Its earliest major growth took place along three socially and geographically different lines. It was played by the athletic gentlemen of London, notably at the Artillery Ground in Finsbury, the White Conduit Club and Thomas Lord's series of three

grounds in the Regents Park-St. John's Wood area. It flourished on the private estates of wealthy patrons in Kent, Sussex and Surrey and, quite independently, on the village greens of Southern England.

In the latter half of the eighteenth century, the Hambledon cricket club rose to considerable eminence. Its doings were evocatively celebrated by one of its players, John Nyren, in a book called *The Young Cricketer's Tutor*. On the basis of ascertainable facts, Hambledon probably was the first example of planned, professional team sport. The club had a number of wealthy members, patrons and backers; but these gentlemen, although many of them were enthusiastic amateurs of the game, barely ventured to appear in the major matches, which were played for vast sums and with considerable side-bets depending on the result. The Hambledon players were drawn from far afield – many of them, from Surrey or Sussex, rode forty or fifty miles in a day, not only for the great matches, but also for practice. These cricketers, countrymen and county-town craftsmen, highly skilled in a country game, exploited, if they did not positively invent, important technical advances in the game – such as the off-break, the use of straight-bat play, fielding tactics and swing ('bias') bowling. By the stern standards of a day when sporting ability was measured by the stakes it won, the professional cricketers of Hambledon earned huge sums of money for their backers.

The windy hills of Hampshire did not appeal to the gentlemen backers: but the professional players were prepared to travel to earn their fees. So by 1800 London – in particular, Lord's Ground – had become the centre of the game. Betting was heavy and corruption was the automatic consequence. In 1817 William Lambert, the finest cricketer of the day, and several other leading players, were barred from cricket for 'selling' a match. Thus cricket went into the Victorian era with the prestige asset of an aura of respectability such as no other popular sport possessed. Its skills were growing sharper: technique was being extended: it was firmly grounded in the public schools and Universities and it was spreading out from London and the South to the Midlands and the North.

One of the strongest – and certainly the oddest – of the reasons for its acceptance in Victorian England was its adoption of the type of social compromise which that age esteemed so highly. While cricket so far surmounted class barriers that the gentlemen-amateurs took the field side by side with the working-class-professionals, the distinction between the two was emphasized by the major match of the season – between 'Gentlemen' and 'Players'.

In the middle of the last century, three distinct but parallel factors further increased the standing of cricket in public esteem. Fresh and strong centres of playing ability emerged in Nottinghamshire, Yorkshire and, later, Lancashire. A one-eyed Nottingham bricklayer and publican, William Clarke, organized the All England XI which travelled the length and breadth of Britain playing local teams of eleven, eighteen and twenty-two for a guaranteed 'gate' and, in doing so, quite incidentally demonstrated and instilled the principles of play throughout the country. Finally, in 1864, William Gilbert Grace, the fifteen-year-old son of a Gloucestershire doctor, scored 170 for South Wales against the Gentlemen of Sussex at Brighton. He was soon to become the ultimate 'eminent Victorian' not only of cricket but of all sport and, until the end of the century, to see 'W. G.' bat was one of the 'sights' to be 'done' – like visiting the Tower of London or Madame Tussaud's.

So at the end of the nineteenth century, the sports and games of England flourished, being still not taken too seriously. In most games the amateurs could match, and sometimes beat, the professionals. Steadily increasing numbers of people played and watched a wide variety of games. America was pre-eminent in boxing and led – though not by an unapproachable margin – in athletics. For the rest, the English could feel that, enjoying their sport, they led the world in ability. The amateur tradition was still strong but already in the realm of international sport which England, almost without knowing it, had fostered, winning was the prime motive. 1900 was, as precisely as one may date historic change, the watershed year: on the backslope lay play: on the side which faced the future, it was competition.

64. *Sussex v. Kent at Brighton, 1849,* from an engraving by S. Lipschitz after drawings by W. Drummond and C. J. Basébe. Ireland's Ground, near St Peter's Church in Brighton, which is shown here, was in fact closed in 1847, two years before the print was published. The match depicted is a purely imaginary one.

THE AMERICAN SCENE

ARTHUR DALEY

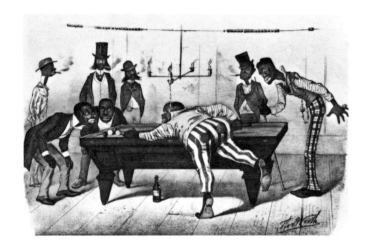

65. *Top Bustin' the Record: Time Knocked Out* by J. Cameron, published by Currier & Ives in 1883. A caricature to commemorate the record-breaking run of the trotter Maud S.

66. *Above Two to Go* by Thomas Worth, published by Currier & Ives in 1882.

It wasn't slow and steady, the rise of American sport during the nineteenth century. It was spectacular. It followed closely on the great surge which, between 1840 and 1880, took America from fifth to first of the world's industrial nations. And it was paralleled, between 1875 and 1900, by a dramatic surge of invention; two inventions, electric light and the camera, were ultimately to sustain and stimulate sport at incredible levels.

Almost all of the American sports were invented, refined or came of age in the second half of the century. The English sports, which were either time-consuming or had limited, 'class' appeal, tended to shrivel away. Some were adapted, along more direct and dynamic lines. One, at least, was an American innovation.

At this time sport was a vitally necessary element in American life. The all-consuming struggle of the early pioneers had long since eased, the excitement of the West had been choked off with the closure of the frontier lands, and there had been a shift from the country to the town and a deluge of European immigrants who sought acceptance in American life, and who brought with them relaxed Sunday traditions.

Puritanism fought to prevent the new permissiveness, but was able at best only to stage a rearguard action. Compromises were made, and one of the more forthright of these was the marriage of a Sunday baseball game with a sacred concert, the band playing in the intervals.

Direct and dynamic. These two words are as adequate as any to describe American sport—indeed, to describe American sport as a mirror of American life. These characteristics made it professional, commercial and crowd-pleasing—facets which serve further to identify the American game of today.

The most American sport, so Mark Twain said, was baseball—for which no further definition is now required than 'the ball game'. Twain said of it: 'Baseball is the very symbol, the outward and visible expression of the drive and push and rush and struggle of the raging, tearing, booming 19th century'.

Popular theory has it that the game was a direct adaptation of the English rounders. It seems more likely, however, that cricket was its source, and that rounders exerted only a small influence. The early settlers came from England with their cricket bats and balls and wickets, but these were soon neglected. There were not the long, leisurely hours which the game required, or the time to cultivate the required stretch of fine turf, and it soon gained the characteristics of modern baseball.

At first the accepted method of dismissing a runner was by hitting him with the thrown ball. As the ball was a hard cricket ball, 'plugging' became unpopular, and it was deemed better to touch—or tag—the runner with the held ball, after it had been thrown to one of the 'bases'. The bases were originally marked with stakes; these also were found to be dangerous, and were replaced with flat stones—ultimately 'plates'.

Cricket expressions were still used, however, in scoring. And it was a group of ex-cricketers who formed themselves, in 1845, into the Knickerbocker Baseball club of New York.

It was the first organization of its kind. They drew up playing rules as well as club statutes, and they produced a plan of a playing area in which the bases were shifted from the box shape into one around which it was easier to run. The new shape was a diamond.

Their first game—the first official baseball game—was against the 'New York Nine'. The Knickerbockers went down by 23–1 in four innings. The winners disbanded and the losers played among themselves for several years. Possibly they displayed better form at post-match banquets than on the diamond. But at least they were causing the 'New York Game' to be better known.

In the 1860s the Brooklyn shipyard men fielded a successful team, the Eckfords, and already the class barrier had been broken. Within a very short space of time ability was going to be a much better credential than breeding—and well rewarded. In fact by that time money was influencing a sport which still claimed to be amateur. Wagering was heavy and the game was falling into disrepute. Then the Cincinnati Red Stockings made a bold move, and one which was to determine the path of the entire sport: they decided to increase their admission charges and to pay their players, writing contracts for a complete season. In short, the players became professionals, and ended the hypocrisy of amateurism.

By the turn of the century, the American ball game had come properly of age. The participants wore knickerbocker trousers, and special, light, studded shoes; the catcher's hands were enclosed in special gloves and his face in a steel mask; the sport had its own glossary of terms. It wasn't a bit like cricket.

There was another English game, a winter game, which was well known in colonial America. This was Soccer. Its main supporters were in the Universities, though the rules varied from state to state. For example, the 'Boston Game' which Harvard started in the 1860s was similar to Rugby football, but produced more kicking than running and tackling. When Harvard arranged a contest with McGill University at Montreal, who played a more orthodox brand

of English Rugby, the two colleges decided to compromise on each set of rules. Harvard liked the Rugby rules, and held out for its new game just when an inter-collegiate body was about to decide on Soccer as the college winter sport. Yale and Princeton followed Harvard's example. The new code was based on orthodox Rugby, but gradually evolved into American football.

From an early stage, stress was placed on brawn; big men were attracted to Yale and Harvard. Yet at the same time the

67. Baseball, c. 1825.

55

this special sphere it took some time for anyone to achieve what the Red Stockings had done for baseball. It finally happened in 1895, when La Trobe, needing a last-minute replacement, hired one from a neighbouring team for $10. Thus was staged the first professional football match. Very soon Pittsburgh was the first city with an all-pro team. The door was open: football, college and professional, swept into the twentieth century.

The original American game, basketball, grew up—like baseball and football—on the Eastern seaboard, not far from where the early British colonialists settled down. Baseball started just over the Hudson River from New York City, in Hoboken; the first football match under modern rules, between Princeton and Rutgers, was held in New Brunswick, New Jersey, less than 50 miles from New York; basketball was born at what is now Springfield College in Massachusetts, 150 miles north of New York City.

Dr. Luther Gulick, head of the athletic department, decided in December 1891 that some indoor sport was necessary to keep the students occupied through the winter months, and he turned to Dr. James Naismith, then a post-graduate student. Naismith, an imaginative fellow, nailed a peach basket to the balcony at either end of the gymnasium floor. The balconies happened to be ten feet above floor level, and the modern steel-rimmed baskets are still at that height. The first game had nine players a side. Later the number was reduced to five and an infinite number of refinements made in rules and skills. Eventually, the game was to be played throughout the world by more nations than any other activity, except soccer football.

Another peculiarly American speciality was harness racing, which utilized the rare breed of horse which trotted or 'paced' rather than galloped. It seems that the nineteenth century American, as well as he liked his sport, liked it even better when he could align it with utility. There is plenty of evidence that the development of light-harness racing horses was regarded, coincidentally, as a means of improving the strains of all types of horses. The family drivers of the day saw them-

68. The Polo Grounds, New York, by T. Fleming, 1887. This famous ground was the home of the New York Baseball Club.

game was developing the feinting, the switches, formations and complex strategical planning which were ultimately to establish it as the doyen of college sports.

Outside of the colleges, too, the sport was taking hold, though it was only after a struggle that fully-fledged professional football won through. The colleges, with their great inducements, offered a virtually professional position, while still holding aloft the banner of amateurism—but away from selves as rather skilled reinsmen as they bowled along the country turnpikes.

The grey harness horses of the American track started with Messenger, a grey stallion foaled in 1780 and brought across from England. He was one of several thoroughbreds imported to inject new blood into the strains produced from European mares, but it was never intended that he should produce that rare specimen, the Trotter. One of his grandsons, Top Gallant, contested the first real race on an American track, at the Hunting Park track, Philadelphia, in 1829. Top Gallant and Whalebone contested a three-heat series in the one afternoon. With one of the heats a tie, they raced four times, which, at four miles for each race, involved in all 16 miles of full-stretch racing.

Previously harness-racing contests had been organized on a 'trial' basis, a champion horse running to settle a wager—to do the mile, for example, in less than 3 minutes. Now, following the Top Gallant-Whalebone contest, match-races gained popularity.

Lady Suffolk was the first of the great trotting mares and won, in the course of an incredible 20-year career, about $100,000 for her owner. The later half of the century was the golden era of the harness horse; with the replacement of the sulky by the trimmer, two-wheeled variety, and pneumatic tyres, the time for the mile came down below the astonishing mark of two minutes.

Golf got off to a later start, but soon flourished, and brought along in its lee the unique American attraction of the Country Club. The sport was introduced by John Reid, a Scot who came to America with a complete set of clubs and plenty of balls. The club which he helped to found at Yonkers was given the name of St Andrews. It was a six-hole course, and the first match played on it was a mixed foursome; women were not be alienated on the sports pitches of America.

Despite some public ridicule for what many Americans regarded as a rather puerile pursuit—this lonely, unemotional progression with a stick and small ball—the first American Open was held in 1895 on a nine-hole course at Newport. It

was decided that the tournament should be open to the world, and the name Open stuck. But although it was always open to all-comers, a foreigner was rarely to win it.

While women shared the honour of christening American golf, they were solely responsible for the introduction of tennis. This sport had gone from England to the West Indies, and was discovered there by a holidaying New York girl. She returned with the necessary equipment, in 1874, and introduced the new game to her friends. But, although her brothers soon became keen and proficient, the sport progressed very slowly as a masculine endeavour. The scoring term 'love' did not endear it to the hardy male sportsman, and prejudice had to be worn down over a long period. Even at the close of the nineteenth century, tennis contained scarcely a hint of the hard battling it offers nowadays.

Boxing was a considerably more manly pastime, and since the late eighteenth century prize-fighting had excited lucky spectators no less in New England than in the Old England, and American boxers presented a serious challenge to England's domination of the sport. Tom Molineaux caused real concern among English patrons, and looked a likely prospect to take the crown from the great Tom Cribb. He might well have done so had he not begun to drink heavily after losing the seventh of his fights in England. He became seriously ill while touring Ireland with a boxing show, and died, sadly, in an army barracks, aged 34.

Boxing was not at this time a gentlemanly sport, and when William Fuller, an English boxer, came to New York in 1826 with a drama group and tried to start a gymnasium and academy for boxing, he created little enthusiasm. The simple truth was that fights were held because large sums of money were wagered. Fuller actually went so far as to declare himself champion of America, but, as an English citizen, he had no claim.

Jacob Hyer, of Dutch stock, is known as the father of American boxing, because the bout in which he defeated Tom Beasley in 1816 was the first in America in which the rules of boxing—as they were then—were observed. His son,

69. *Top A Disputed Heat: Claiming a Foul* by Thomas Worth, published by Currier & Ives in 1878.

70. *Above* A football match between Yale and Princeton, November 27th, 1879, by A. B. Frost.

final successful defence–a 75-round epic with Jake Kilrain–was the last bare-knuckled fight on turf. The new champion was known as 'Gentleman Jim'. Compared to most of his predecessors, who had scorned a conventionally decent life, Corbett was a straightforward citizen as well as a class boxer. Removed from its bar-room image, boxing won the support of better-class patrons, and became respectable.

If the rise of American sport through the nineteenth century was dynamic and heady, it also precipitated the inevitable abuses that result from professionalism in sport. In college football, which should have been a wholesome enough sphere, there were reports of brutality and scandalous recruiting. It was said that Yale acquired one James Hogan by offering him a hotel suite, a trip to Cuba, free tuition, a monopoly on the sale of score-cards and a job. John L. Sullivan made use of his fame by stage appearances and through advertising. Other boxers contracted themselves to photographers. Tom Sayers, immediately after one fight, shouted to photographers: 'It's no good, gentlemen. I've gone and sold my mug to Mr. Newbold.'

71. *The Close of the Battle, or the Champion Triumphant*. The American Molineaux fought Cribb, the Champion of England, at Thistleton-Gap in Cumberland on September 28th, 1811. The fight attracted a great deal of attention, and a crowd of over 20,000 assembled. They were not disappointed; it was a classic match which eventually ended, after 55 minutes, in victory for Cribb.

Tom, thrashed Yankee Sullivan in 1849, for $10,000 a side, and is regarded as the first American champion.

However the sport of boxing, and the interest in it, depended not so much on the fate of championship crowns, but on the intensity of personal issues, on wagering, and often on barbarism. The bare-knuckle fighters were a tough breed. One Irish boxer and champion of America, Jim Elliott, was twice imprisoned, and finally died in a gun brawl in a saloon. Yet another met his death in a saloon, another shot himself, and one died mysteriously in prison.

Gradually the precedence in world boxing–such as it was–swung to America, and the heavyweight champion of the 1890s, James J. Corbett, was widely recognized as the world champion. Corbett won the title from John L. Sullivan, whose

58

ANGLING

HONEST, CIVIL, QUIET MEN

From *The Compleat Angler* by Izaak Walton, 1653

PISCATOR. And now you shall see me try my skill to catch a Trout; and at my next walking, either this evening or to-morrow morning, I will give you direction how you yourself shall fish for him.

VENATOR. Trust me, master, I see now it is a harder matter to catch a Trout than a Chub; for I have put on patience, and followed you these two hours, and not seen a fish stir, neither at your minnow or your worm.

PISCATOR. Well, scholar, you must endure worse luck sometime, or you will never make a good angler. But what say you now? there is a Trout now, and a good one too, if I can but hold him; and two or three turns more will tire him. Now you see he lies still, and the sleight is to land him: reach me that landing-net. So, Sir, now he is mine own: what say you now, is not this worth all my labour and your patience?

VENATOR. On my word, master, this is a gallant Trout; what shall we do with him?

PISCATOR. Marry, e'en eat him to supper: we'll go to my hostess from whence we came; she told me, as I was going out of door, that my brother Peter, a good angler and a cheerful companion, had sent word he would lodge there to-night, and bring a friend with him. My hostess has two beds, and I know you and I may have the best: we'll rejoice with my brother Peter and his friend, tell tales, or sing ballads, or make a catch, or find some harmless sport to content us, and pass away a little time without offence to God or man.

VENATOR. A match, good master, let's go to that house, for the linen looks white, and smells of lavender, and I long to lie in a pair of sheets that smell so. Let's be going, good master, for I am hungry again with fishing.

PISCATOR. Nay, stay a little, good scholar. I caught my last Trout with a worm; now I will put on a minnow, and try a quarter of an hour about yonder trees for another; and, so, walk towards our lodging. Look you, scholar, thereabout we shall have a bite presently, or not at all. Have with you, Sir: o' my word I have hold of him. Oh! it is a great logger-headed Chub; come, hang him upon that willow twig, and let's be going. But turn out of the way a little, good scholar! towards yonder high honeysuckle hedge; there we'll sit and sing, whilst this shower falls so gently upon the teeming earth, and gives yet a sweeter smell to the lovely flowers that adorn these verdant meadows.

72. *Left False Perspective* by William Hogarth, 1753.

73. *Above* Even in the 1820s fishing rights were jealously guarded, and trespassers liable for prosecution. In this case the angler is just about to be punished with a ducking.

dams. As I thus sat, these and other sights had so fully possest my soul with content, that I thought, as the poet has happily exprest it,

'I was for that time lifted above earth;
And possest joys not promis'd in my birth.'

As I left this place, and entered into the next field, a second pleasure entertained me; 'twas a handsome milk-maid, that had not yet attained so much age and wisdom as to load her mind with any fears of many things that will never be, as too many men too often do; but she cast away all care, and sung like a nightingale. Her voice was good, and the ditty fitted for it; it was that smooth song which was made by Kit Marlow, now at least fifty years ago; and the milk-maid's mother sung an answer to it, which was made by Sir Walter Raleigh, in his younger days. They were old-fashioned poetry, but choicely good; I think much better than the strong lines that are now in fashion in this critical age. Look yonder! on my word, yonder, they both be a-milking again. I will give her the Chub, and persuade them to sing those two songs to us.

God speed you, good woman! I have been a-fishing; and am going to Bleak Hall to my bed; and having caught more fish than will sup myself and my friend, I will bestow this upon you and your daughter, for I use to sell none.

MILK-WOMAN. Marry! God requite you, Sir, and we'll eat it cheerfully. And if you come this way a-fishing two months hence, a grace of God! I'll give you a syllabub of new verjuice, in a new-made hay-cock, for it. And my Maudlin shall sing you one of her best ballads; for she and I both love all anglers, they be such honest, civil, quiet men.

74. Fishing from a boat, by Henry Alken, c. 1818.

Look! under that broad beech-tree I sat down, when I was last this way a-fishing; and the birds in the adjoining grove seemed to have a friendly contention with an echo, whose dead voice seemed to live in a hollow tree near to the brow of that primrose-hill. There I sat viewing the silver streams glide silently towards their centre, the tempestuous sea; yet sometimes opposed by rugged roots and pebble-stones, which broke their waves, and turned them into foam; and sometimes I beguiled time by viewing the harmless lambs; some leaping securely in the cool shade, whilst others sported themselves in the cheerful sun; and saw others craving comfort from the swollen udders of their bleating

LET ME LIVE HARMLESSLY

From *The Compleat Angler* by Izaak Walton, 1653

Let me live harmlessly, and near the brink
    Of Trent or Avon have a dwelling-place;
Where I may see my quill, or cork, down sink
    With eager bite of Perch, or Bleak, or Dace;
And on the world and my Creator think:
    Whilst some men strive ill-gotten goods t' embrace;
And others spend their time in base excess
Of wine, or worse, in war and wantonness.

Let them that list, these pastimes still pursue,
  And on such pleasing fancies feed their fill;
So I the fields and meadows green may view,
  And daily by fresh rivers walk at will,
Among the daisies and the violets blue,
  Red hyacinth, and yellow daffodil,
Purple Narcissus like the morning rays,
Pale gander-grass, and azure culver-keys.

I count it higher pleasure to behold
  The stately compass of the lofty sky;
And in the midst thereof, like burning gold,
  The flaming chariot of the world's great eye;
The watery clouds that in the air up-roll'd
  With sundry kinds of painted colours fly;
And fair Aurora, lifting up her head,
Still blushing, rise from old Tithonus' bed.

The hills and mountains raised from the plains,
  The plains extended level with the ground,
The grounds divided into sundry veins,
  The veins inclos'd with rivers running round;
These rivers making way through nature's chains,
  With headlong course, into the sea profound;
The raging sea, beneath the vallies low,
Where lakes, and rills, and rivulets do flow.

The lofty woods, the forests wide and long,
  Adorned with leaves and branches fresh and green,
In whose cool bowers the birds with many a song
  Do welcome with their quire the summer's Queen;
The meadows fair, where Flora's gifts, among
  Are intermixt, with verdant grass between;
The silver-scaled fish that softly swim
Within the sweet brook's crystal, watery stream.

All these, and many more of his creation
  That made the heavens, the Angler oft doth see;
Taking therein no little delectation,
  To think how strange, how wonderful they be:

Framing thereof an inward contemplation
  To set his heart from other fancies free;
And whilst he looks on these with joyful eye,
His mind is rapt above the starry sky.

ARCHERY

PHILOLOGE TO SHOOTE STREYGHT

From *Toxophilus* by Roger Ascham, 1545

The diversitie of mens standyng and drawing causeth diverse men to loke at theyr marke diverse wayes: yet they al lede a mans hand to shoote streyght yf nothyng els stoppe. So that cumlynesse is the only judge of best lokyng at the marke. Some men wonder why in casting a mans eye at ye marke, the hand should go streyght. Surely ye he consydered the nature of a mans eye, he wolde not wonder at it: For this I am certayne of, that no servaunt to hys mayster, no chylde to hys father is so obedient, as everye joynte and pece of the body is to do what soever the eye biddes. The eye is the guide, the ruler and the succourer of al the other partes. The hande, the foote and other members dare do nothynge without the eye, as doth appere on the night and darke corners. The eye is the very tonge wherwith wyt and reason doth speke to every parte of the body, and the wyt doth not so sone signifye a thynge by the eye, as every parte is redye to folow, or rather prevent the byddyng of the eye. Thys is playne in many thinges, but most evident in sence and seyghtynge, as I have heard men saye. There every parte standynge in feare to have a blowe, runnes to the eye for helpe, as yonge chyldren do to ye mother: the foote, the hand, and al wayteth upon the eye. Yf the eye byd ye hand either beare of, or smite, or the foote either go forward, or backeward, it doth so: And that whyche is

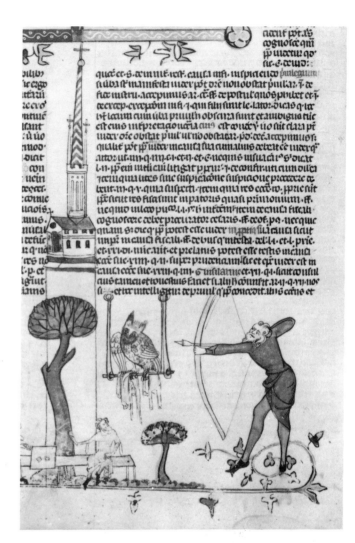

75. Archery, from the *Queen Mary Psalter*, c. 1310.

moost wonder of all the one man lookynge stedfastly at the other mans eye and not at his hand, wyl, even as it were, rede in his eye where he purposeth to smyte nexte, for the eye is nothyng els but a certayne wyndowe for wit to shote oute hir head at.

Thys wonderfull worke of god in makynge all the members so obedient to the eye, is a pleasaunte thynge to remember and loke upon: therefore an Archer maye be sure in learnyng to looke at hys marke when he is yong, always to shoote streyghte. The thynges that hynder a man whyche looketh at hys marke, to shote streyght, be these: A syde wynde, a bowe either to stronge, or els to weake, an ill arme, whan the fether runneth on the bowe to much, a byg brested shafte, for hym that shoteth under hande, bycause it wyll hobble: a little brested shafte for hym yat shoteth above ye hande, bycause it wil starte: a payre of windynge prickes, and many other thinges mo, which you shal marke your selfe, and as ye knowe them, so learne to amend them. If a man woulde leave to looke at his shafte, and learne to loke at his marke, he maye use this waye, whiche a good shooter tolde me ones that he did. Let him take his bowe on the nyght, and shoote at ii. lightes, and there he shall be compelled to looke always at his marke, and never at his shafte: This thing ones or twyse used wyl cause hym forsake lokynge at hys shafte. Yet let hym take hede of settynge his shafte in the bowe.

Thus Philologe to shoote streyght is the leaste maysterie of all, yf a manne order hym selfe thereafter, in hys youthe. And as for keypynge a lengthe, I am sure the rules whiche I gave you, will never disceyve you, so that there shal lacke nothynge, eyther of hittinge the marke alwayes, or elles verye nere shotynge, excepte the faulte be onely in youre owne selfe, whiche maye come ii wayes, eyther in having a faynt harte or courage, or elles in sufferynge your selfe over muche to be led with affection: yf a mans mynde fayle hym, the bodye whiche is ruled by the mynde, can never do his duetie, yf lacke of courage were not, men myght do mo mastries than they do, as doeth appere in leapynge and vaultinge.

All affections and specially anger, hurteth bothe mynde and bodye. The mynde is blynde therby: and yf the mynde be blynde, it can not rule the bodye aright. The body both blood and bone, as they say, is brought out of his ryght course by anger: Wherby a man lacketh his right strengthe, and therfore can not shoote wel. Yf these thynges be avoyded (wherof I wyll speake no more, both bycause they belong not properly to shoting, and also you can teach me better, in them, than I you) and al the preceptes whiche I have gyven you, dilligently marked, no doubt ye shal shoote as well as ever man dyd yet, by the grace of God.

76. Frontispiece to *Sporting Anecdotes* by Pierce Egan, 1825. Pierce Egan was the outstanding sporting journalist of the 19th century, and spent most of his life travelling round the country to sporting events of every description. He was the author of *Boxiana*, published in parts in 1812–13.

BOXING

THE GAS-MAN AND BILL NEATE

From *The Fight* by William Hazlitt, 1816

Reader, have you ever seen a fight? If not, you have a pleasure to come, at least if it is a fight like that between the Gas-man and Bill Neate. The crowd was very great when we arrived on the spot; open carriages were coming up, with streamers flying and music playing, and the country-people were pouring in over hedge and ditch in all directions, to see their hero beat or be beaten. The odds were still on Gas, but only about five to four. Gully had been down to try Neate, and had backed him considerably, which was a damper to the sanguine confidence of the adverse party. About two hundred thousand pounds were pending. The Gas says, he has lost 3000*l*. which were promised him by different gentlemen if he had won. He had presumed too much on himself, which

6. THE GREAT FIGHT BETWEEN BROOME AND HANNAN FOR £1000

From a print after H. Heath, engraved by C. Hunt. 22ins × 18½ins

The fight between John Broome (on the left) and John Hannan, for £1000 and the lightweight championship of England, took place on January 26th 1841, at New Park Farm, Beeston, Oxfordshire, on the Buckinghamshire border. It lasted for one hour nineteen minutes – forty-seven rounds (a round was then ended by a knockdown). Broome's greater strength began to tell after an hour of 'violent milling'. At the beginning of the forty-seventh round, Hannan had been weakening for some time, and taking heavy punishment. He tried to rise from the knee of his second, then suddenly fell forward unconscious on the turf, and Broome was awarded the prize and the championship. He was not the only fighter of his family – his brother Harry was a middleweight, and Broome trained him up to be heavyweight champion of England. This fight was John Hannan's last, but it was not the end of his public career, for he built up a new reputation by becoming a celebrated teacher of boxing.

As was customary at the time, there are two roped squares. Privileged spectators were allowed inside the outer ropes, while the general public were outside – kept there, if necessary, by the whippers. On this occasion the distance between the two sets of ropes was unusually large (20 yards).

THE GREAT FIGHT

BETWEEN BROOME AND HANNAN FOR £1000,

Which took place Jan.ʸ 26.ᵗʰ 1841, in the presence of Thousands of Spectators, at New Park Farm, near Bicester, Oxon, on the borders of Buckinghamshire.

THE BATTLE LASTED 1 HOUR AND 19 MINUTES,   47 ROUNDS,   WHEN BROOME WAS DECLARED THE VICTOR.

had made others presume on him. This spirited and formidable young fellow seems to have taken for his motto the old maxim, that 'there are three things necessary to success in life – *Impudence! Impudence! Impudence!*' It is so in matters of opinion, but not in the FANCY, which is the most practical of all things, though even here confidence is half the battle, but only half. Our friend had vapoured and swaggered too much, as if he wanted to grin and bully his adversary out of the fight. 'Alas! the Bristol man was so tamed!' – 'This is *the grave-digger*' (would Tom Hickman exclaim in the moments of intoxication from gin and success, shewing his tremendous right hand), 'this will send many of them to their long homes; I haven't done with them yet!' Why should he – though he had licked four of the best men within the hour, yet why should he threaten to inflict dishonourable chastisement on my old master Richmond, a veteran going off the stage and who has borne his sable honours meekly? Magnanimity, my dear Tom, and bravery, should be inseparable. Or why should he go up to his antagonist, the first time he ever saw him at the Fives Court, and measuring him from head to foot with a glance of contempt, as Achilles surveyed Hector, say to him, 'What, are you Bill Neate? I'll knock more blood out of that great carcase of thine, this day fortnight, than you ever knock'd out of a bullock's!' It was not manly, 'twas not fighter-like. If he was sure of the victory (as he was not), the less said about it the better. Modesty should accompany the FANCY as its shadow. The best men were always the best behaved. Jem Belcher, the Game Chicken (before whom the Gas-man could not have lived) were civil, silent men. So is Cribb, so is Tom Belcher, the most elegant of sparrers, and not a man for every one to take by the nose. I enlarged on this topic in the mail (while Turtle was asleep), and said very wisely (as I thought) that impertinence was a part of no profession. A boxer was bound to beat his man, but not to thrust his fist, either actually or by implication, in every one's face. Even a highwayman, in the way of trade, may blow out your brains, but if he uses foul language at the same time, I should say he was no gentleman. A boxer, I would infer, need not be a blackguard or a coxcomb, more than another. Perhaps I press this point too much on a fallen man – Mr. Thomas Hickman has by this time learnt that first of all lessons, 'That man was made to mourn.' He has lost nothing by the late fight but his presumption; and that every man may do as well without! By an over-display of this quality, however, the public had been prejudiced against him, and the *knowing-ones* were taken in. Few but those who had bet on him wished Gas to win. With my own prepossessions on the subject, the result of the 11th of December appeared to

me as fine a piece of poetical justice as I had ever witnessed. The difference of weight between the two combatants (14 stone to 12) was nothing to the sporting men. Great, heavy, clumsy, long-armed Bill Neate kicked the beam in the scale of the Gas-man's vanity. The amateurs were frightened at his big words, and thought they would make up for the difference of six feet and five feet nine. Truly, the FANCY are not men of imagination. They judge of what has been, and

77. J. Randall and E. Turner sparring at the Fives Court, by T. Blake, engraved by C. Turner and published in 1821. The Fives Court was in James Street, Haymarket, and was a great rendezvous of the Fancy.

mid-day sun. For it was now noon, and we had an hour to wait. This is the trying time. It is then the heart sickens, as you think what the two champions are about, and how short a time will determine their fate. After the first blow is struck, there is no opportunity for nervous apprehensions; you are swallowed up in the immediate interest of the scene – but

> 'Between the acting of a dreadful thing
> And the first motion, all the interim is
> Like a phantasma, or a hideous dream.'

I found it so as I felt the sun's rays clinging to my back, and saw the white wintry clouds sink below the verge of the horizon. 'So, I thought, my fairest hopes have faded from my sight! – so will the Gas-man's glory, or that of his adversary, vanish in an hour.'

CHAMPIONS OF THE RING

From *Boxiana* by Pierce Egan, 1818-24

Previous to the days of BROUGHTON it was downright *slaughtering*, – or, in the modern acceptation, either *gluttony*, *strength*, or *bottom*, decided almost every contest. But after BROUGHTON appeared as a professor of the gymnastic art, he drew crowds after him to witness his exhibitions; there was a *neatness* about his method completely new, and unknown to his auditors – he *stopped* the blows aimed at any part of him by his antagonist, with so much skill, and *hit* his man away with so much ease, that he astonished and terrified his opponents beyond measure; and those persons who had the temerity to enter the lists with BROUGHTON were soon convinced of his superior knowledge and athletic prowess: and most of his competitors, who were compelled to *give in* from their exhausted and beaten state, had the mortification to behold BROUGHTON scarcely touched, and to appear with as much cheerfulness and indifference as if he had never been engaged in a *set-to*.

He was indebted to nature for a good person; his countenance was manly and open; and, possessing a sharp and penetrating eye, that almost looked through the object before him, gave a fine animation to his face. His form was athletic and commanding; there was an importance about it which denoted uncommon strength, and which every spectator felt impressed with that beheld him. Six feet, wanting an inch,

78. Southwark Fair, by William Hogarth, 1733, where James Figg kept a booth which was patronized by both the aristocracy and the more lowly followers of pugilism. The spectators were entertained by fencing, backsword, cudgeling and boxing exhibitions.

cannot conceive of anything that is to be. The Gas-man had won hitherto; therefore he must beat a man half as big again as himself – and that to a certainty. Besides, there are as many feuds, factions, prejudices, pedantic notions in the FANCY as in the state or in the schools. Mr. Gully is almost the only cool, sensible man among them, who exercises an unbiased discretion, and is not a slave to his passions in these matters. But enough of reflections, and to our tale. The day, as I have said, was fine for a December morning. The grass was wet, and the ground miry, and ploughed up with multitudinous feet, except that, within the ring itself, there was a spot of virgin-green closed in and unprofaned by vulgar tread, that shone with dazzling brightness in the

in height; and fourteen stone, or thereabouts, in weight.

BROUGHTON became as a *fixed star* in the pugilistic hemisphere; his talents as a Boxer gained him many admirers and patrons; but his good temper, generosity of disposition, and gentleness of manners, ensured him numerous friends. He was intelligent, communicative, and not destitute of wit. The system he laid down was plain, and easy to be understood; and under his instruction, several of his pupils arrived at a pugilistic eminence, and gave distinguished proofs of the acquirements they had gained under so great a master.

Notwithstanding the inferiority of Boxers, previous to the days of BROUGHTON, it may not be improper, as far as they can be traced with any degree of accuracy, so as to render the connection more complete and strong, to give some short account of their feats.

SOUTHWARK FAIR, during its continuance, was an uncommon scene of attraction to the inhabitants in, and contiguous to, London, from the various sports and pastimes which were exhibited by its versatility of performers. Boxing and cudgelling were strong features among the other amusements: refinement, it appears, was not so well understood *then* as at the present period; although several of the most celebrated actors of that day, did not feel *ashamed* to make known their efforts to amuse the populace. When even the stage was not considered in a degenerate state, and while the irresistible and loud roars of laughter prevailed outside of the booths, from an intermixture of all ranks of people, the involuntary tear was seen stealing down the cheeks of the audiences within, at the imaginary sufferings of the hero or heroine, from the excellent *manner* in which it was *told*. Genius and talent was often seen, felt, and acknowledged, under many of those ragged coverings; however difficult it may be to experience under more classic and magnificent domes, the *mere* hint at such things now-a-days, would make our fixed theatrical star

JOHN KEMBLE –
Tremble!

Nor did that truly great Colossus of Literature (Dr. Johnson) appear shy, in witnessing the eccentricities developed by human beings at such places of amusement, where the finest display of NATURE and ART that could be experienced, were to be seen *contrasted*, and REAL LIFE, in all its abundant varieties, portrayed in its native dress. To a *mind* like that of Dr. Johnson's, few circumstances escaped his notice, whether attracted by the loud laugh at the rude and noisy fair, or the *self-approving* smile at the more refined and splendid chateau; in the manly

display of the pugilist, or in appealing eloquence of the orator, it was appreciated and treasured up, added to his midnight sallies with the unfortunate and pitiable Savage, united with his intellectual acquirements; and which, doubtless, formed the *stamina* of those works that have tended to add so much literary reputation to this country.

The learned Doctor, in himself, was another *striking* proof of pugilism being a national trait, by having a regular set-to with an athletic brewer's servant, who had insulted him in Fleet-street, and gave the fellow a complete milling in a few minutes.

BOXING and CUDGELLING, it appeared, degenerated into down-right ferocity and barbarity at this fair, from the drunkenness and inequality of the combatants, and the various artifices adopted to get money, which at last became so disgusting, that it was declared a public nuisance, and in 1743 Southwark fair was suppressed.

79. *Top left* John Broughton, by William Hogarth, 1742. John Broughton, the 'Father of Boxing', was probably the greatest bare-knuckle prize-fighter in history. He also contributed much to the organization of boxing, and in 1743 drew up the first code of rules governing the sport.

80. *Above* Handbill of a fight between Jem Ward and Jack Carter. Ward was a prize-fighter from Bow, in London, who became Champion of England in 1825. In this fight, which took place in about 1821, Ward was beaten, but he later successfully defended his title against Jack Carter, and retired undefeated.

their experience and observations, for my part I shall be free and scorn to conceal anything that may tend to the propagation of the art and mystery of cock-fighting; wherefore as to the dyeting and ordering of fighting cocks take these instructions following.

The time of taking up your cocks is about the latter end of August, for from that time till the latter end of May cocking is seasonable and in request, the summer season being improper by reason of its great heat.

Having taken them up, view them well, and see that they are sound, hard feather'd, and full summ'd, that is having all their feathers compleat, then put them into several pens, having a moving perch therein, so set it at which corner of the perch you think most convenient; the fashion and form of these pens you may have at the house of any cocker, and therefore I shall give you no directions how to make them, only be advised to keep your pens clean, and let your cocks want either meat or water.

7. A FROLIC HOME AFTER A BLANK DAY

From a drawing by John Leech, c. 1860. 24¾ins × 16½ins

This drawing is taken from Leech's *The Noble Science of Incidents of the Hunting Field*, and was exhibited in 1862 as one of a series of *Sketches in Oils*. Leech was himself a keen huntsman, known as a timid but enthusiastic rider. He learned to ride at six years old, and did most of his hunting with the Puckeridge, in Hertfordshire. The background of his pictures is typical Puckeridge country – 'regular plough country, often with straggling wattle fences set on low banks and accompanied by good-sized ditches . . . round corn stacks and weatherboard barns with tiled roofs'. This particular one was originally a woodcut done for *Punch*, the magazine for which Leech did much of his work, and one can see, on the flanks of the horse jibbing at the hurdle, that the rough shading marks of the woodcut have not been removed. The sheepfold that worries the horse so much was once a familiar feature of that part of the country, and indeed of all the English countryside, but now sheepfolds, like shepherds, are dying out.

Leech was highly regarded as an artist in his own time. He was originally put to medical studies at St Bartholomews Hospital, but gained nothing from this but a marked skill in anatomical drawing. Then, when his Irish father failed in business, he had to take to book illustration. Many of the books he illustrated were not worth his talents, but being fortunate – and unusual – in combining the assets of industry and charm, he soon became well known, as a *Punch* artist and as the illustrator of Jorrocks and of Dickens' *A Christmas Carol*. Dickens was one of his close friends, as were the painter Millais and William Makepiece Thackeray, who wrote of Leech's work: 'The outdoor sketcher will not fail to remark the excellent fidelity with which Mr Leech draws the background of his little pictures. The homely landscape, the sea, the winter wood by which the huntsmen ride, the light and clouds, the birds floating overhead, are indicated by a few strokes which show the artist's untiring watchfulness and love of nature. He is a natural truthteller, and indulges in no flights of fancy. He loves horses, dogs, river and field sports.'

81. *Above* Cock-fighting, 1822. Before the development of boxing and horse-racing, cock-fighting provided the chief means of gambling, and cocking-mains were often combined with race meetings. From *The Annals of Sporting and Fancy Gazette, Vol. 1.*

82. *Top right* Pit ticket for a cock-fight, by William Hogarth, c.1725.

COCK-FIGHTING

OF DIETING AND ORDERING A COCK FOR BATTEL

From *The Compleat Gamester* by Charles Cotton, 1674

In the dieting and ordering of a cock for battail consisteth all the substance of profit and pleasure; and therefore your cunning cock merchants are very cautious of divulging the secrets (as they call them) of dieting, for on that depends the winning or losing of the battel, they knowing very well that the best cock undieted is unable to encounter the worst that is dyeted; let others be as niggardly as they please of

A Frolic Home after a Blank Day

For the first four days after your cock is pend, feed him with the crumbs of old manchet cut into square bits about a handful at a time, and feed him thrice a day therewith, that is at sun-rising, when the sun is in his meridian, and at sun-setting, and let his water be from the coldest spring you can get it.

Having fed your cock thus four days, or so long till you think he hath purg'd himself of his corn, worms, gravel, and other coarse feeding, then in the morning take him out of his pen and let him sparr a while with another cock. Sparring is after this manner. Cover each of your cocks heels with a pair of Hots made of bombasted rolls of leather, so covering the spurs that they cannot bruise or wound one another, and so setting them down on straw in a room, or green grass abroad, let them fight a good while, but by no means suffer them to draw blood of one another; the benefit that accrues hereby is this, it heateth and chafeth their bodies, and it breaketh the fat and the glut that is within them, and adapts it for purgation.

Having sparred as much as is sufficient, which you may know when you see them pant and grow weary, then take them up, and taking off their Hots give them a Diaphoretick or sweating after this manner. You must put them in deep straw-baskets made for the purpose, or for want

of them take a couple of cocking-bags and fill them with straw half ways, then put in your cocks severally, and cover them over with straw to the top, then shut down the lids and let them sweat; but do not forget to give them first some white sugar-candy, chopt Rosemary, and butter mingled and incorporated together, let the quantity be about the bigness of a walnut, by so doing you will cleanse him of his grease, increase his strength and prolong his breath.

THE COCKING-MAIN

From *Life on the Mississippi* by Mark Twain, 1883

We went to a cockpit in New Orleans on a Saturday afternoon. I had never seen a cock-fight before. There were men and boys there of all ages and all colours, and of many languages and nationalities. But I noticed one quite conspicuous and surprising absence: the traditional brutal faces. There were no brutal faces. With no cock-fighting going on, you could have played the gathering on a stranger for a prayer-meeting; and after it began, for a revival – provided you blindfolded your stranger – for the shouting was something prodigious.

A negro and a white man were in the ring; everybody else outside. The cocks were brought in in sacks; and when time was called, they were taken out by the two bottle-holders, stroked, caressed, poked toward each other, and finally liberated. The big black cock plunged instantly at the little grey one and struck him on the head with his spur. The grey responded with spirit. Then the Babel of many-tongued shoutings broke out, and ceased not thenceforth. When the cocks had been fighting some little time, I was expecting them momently to drop dead, for both were blind, red with blood, and so exhausted that they frequently fell down. Yet they would not give up, neither would they die. The negro and the white man would pick them up every few seconds, wipe them off, blow cold water on them in a fine spray, and take their heads in their mouths and hold them there a moment – to warm back the perishing life perhaps; I do not know. Then, being set down again, the dying creatures would totter gropingly about, with dragging wings, find each other, strike a guess-work blow or two, and fall exhausted once more.

I did not see the end of the battle. I forced myself to endure it as long as I could, but it was too pitiful a sight; so I made frank confession to that effect, and we retired. We heard afterward that the black cock died in the ring, and fighting to the last.

83. *Left The Royal Cock Pit* by Thomas Rowlandson, published in 1808 for the *Microcosm of London*. The Royal Cock Pit, in Birdcage Walk, Whitehall, was built by Henry VIII, who was a keen patron of the sport: through his support, and that of the Stuart kings, it came to be known as 'the royal diversion'.

84. *Above Old Trodgon* by Robert Hodgson, c. 1789. A celebrated fighting cock trained by B. Robson. According to the caption, he won £50 in 1785, £100 in 1786 and £200 in 1787. The vicious, curved spurs were fitted over the cock's natural spurs: they were more dangerous, but inflicted cleaner wounds than the natural spur, which seems to carry some poison.

TRICKS OF THE TRADE

From The Cricket Field *by James Pycroft, 1851*

'You see, sir,' said one fine old man, with brilliant eye and quickness of movement, that showed his right hand had not yet forgot its cunning, 'matches were bought, and matches were sold, and gentlemen who meant honestly lost large sums of money, till the rogues beat themselves at last. They overdid it; they spoilt their own trade; and, as I said to one of them, 'a knave and a fool makes a bad partnership; so, you and yourself will never prosper.' Well, surely there was robbery enough: and, not a few of the great players earned money to their own disgrace; but, if you'll believe me, there was not half the selling there was said to

8. THE ROYAL ACADEMY CLUB IN MARYLEBONE FIELDS

From a print after Francis Hayman, RA, engraved by C. Grignion and published on July 16th, 1748. 23¾ins × 18ins

Cricket clubs as such were very few before 1750, though social clubs – the Englishman has always been a clubbish animal – were plentiful enough, and their members would sometimes indulge in the fashionable sport of cricket, already patronized by some of the most influential persons in the land. The mode of dress for cricketers was not very different from a player's normal attire, the cumbersome accoutrements merely being discarded: tight (usually coloured) breeches, silk stockings and buckled shoes, full-sleeved shirts and neat jockey caps. The umpires wore laced cocked hats and full-skirted coats, and each carried a cricket bat which the batsman, when running, had to touch to make good his ground. The bat was curved at the striking end like an old-fashioned dinner knife – it was of one piece and, to our eyes, a clumsy weapon. It defended a wicket of two stumps and one bail on a pitch, most often rough and bumpy, twenty-two yards long – as it is today. All bowling was underarm, along the ground and generally quick. The over was of four balls, and pads and gloves were unknown, as were leg-before-wicket decisions and the follow-on. The scorers sat in splendid prominence (right foreground) notching or carving the runs on sticks, a primitive but effective method of recording the day's proceedings.

Very soon 'length' bowling became popular, with the straight bat and third stump. But even by the 1740s a code of laws was in use that was not so very far removed from that used today, and cricket had already gripped the imagination in a way that was to ensure for it its honoured place as England's premier game.

Evidently there is abundant fascination about this 'sport' for such as have had a degree of familiarity with it. I never saw people enjoy anything more than this gathering enjoyed this fight. The case was the same with old grey-heads and with boys of ten. They lost themselves in frenzies of delight. The 'cocking-main' is an inhuman sort of entertainment, there is no question about that; still, it seems a much more respectable and far less cruel sport than fox-hunting – for the cocks like it; they experience, as well as confer enjoyment; which is not the fox's case.

85. Cricket in the early 18th century.

Cricket.

be. Yes, I can guess, sir, much as you have been talking to all the old players over this good stuff, (pointing to the brandy and water I had provided) no doubt you have heard that B – – sold as bad as the rest. I'll tell the truth: one match up the country I did sell, – a match made by Mr. Osbaldeston at Nottingham. I had been sold out of a match just before, and lost 10l., and happening to hear it I joined two others of our eleven to sell, and get back my money. I won 10l. exactly, and of this roguery no one ever suspected me; but many was the time I have been blamed for selling when as innocent as a babe. In those days, when so much money was on the matches, every man who lost his money would blame some one. Then, if A missed a catch, or B made no runs, – and where's the player whose hand is always in? – that man was called a rogue directly. So, when a man was doomed to lose his character and to bear all the smart, there was the more temptation to do like others, and after 'the kicks' to come in for 'the halfpence.' But I am an old man now, and heartily sorry I have been ever since: because, but for that Nottingham match, I could have said with a clear conscience to a gentleman like you, that all that was said was false, and I never sold a match in my life; but now I can't. But, if I had fifty sons, I would never put one of them, for all the games in the world, in the way of the roguery that I have witnessed. The temptation was really very great, – too great by far for any poor man to be exposed to, – no richer than ten shillings a week, let alone harvest time. – I never told you, sir, the way I first was brought to London. I was a lad of eighteen at this Hampshire

village, and Lord Winchelsea had seen us play among ourselves, and watched the match with the Hambledon Club on Broad-halfpenny, when I scored forty-three against David Harris, and ever so many of the runs against David's bowling, and no one ever could manage David before. So, next year, in the month of March, I was down in the meadows, when a gentleman came across the field with Farmer Hilton: and, thought I, all in a minute, now this is something about cricket. Well, at last it was settled I was to play Hampshire against England, at London, in White-Conduit-Fields ground, in the month of June. For three months I did nothing but think about that match. Tom Walker was to travel up from this county, and I agreed to go with him, and found myself at last with a merry company of cricketers, – all the men, whose names I had ever heard as foremost in the game – met together drinking, card-playing, betting and singing at the Green Man (that was the great cricketer's house), in Oxford Street, – no man without his wine, I assure you, and such suppers as three guineas a game to lose, and five to win (that was then the sum for players) could never pay for long. To go to London by the waggon, earn five guineas three or four times told, and come back with half the money in your pocket to the plough again, was all very well talking. You know what young folk are, sir, when they get together: mischief brews stronger in large quantities: so, many spent all their earnings, and were soon glad to make more money some other way. Hundreds of pounds were bet upon all the great matches, and other wagers laid on the scores of the finest players, and that too by men who had a book for every race and every match in the sporting world; men who lived by gambling; and, as to honesty, gambling and honesty don't often go together. What was easier, then, than for such sharp gentlemen to mix with the players, take advantage of their difficulties, and say, 'your backers, my Lord this, and the Duke of that, sell matches and over-rule all your good play, so why shouldn't you have a share of the plunder?' – That was their constant argument. 'Serve them as they serve you.' – You have heard of Jim Bland, the turfsman, and his brother Joe – two nice boys. When Jemmy Dawson was hanged for poisoning the horse, the Blands never felt safe till the rope was round Dawson's neck: to keep him quiet, they persuaded him to the last hour that no one dared hang him; and a certain nobleman had a reprieve in his pocket. Well, one day in April, Joe Bland traced me out in this parish, and tried his game on with me. 'You may make a fortune,' he said, 'if you will listen to me: so much for the match with Surrey, and so much more for the Kent match –' 'Stop,' said I: 'Mr. Bland, you talk too fast; I am rather too old for this trick; you never buy

86. *Left* Cricket match, from *A Few Recollections of Eton*, published in 1840.

87 and 88. Alfred Mynn (*top*) and Charles George Taylor, by C. J. Basébe, engraved by Charles Hunt and published in c. 1850. Two prominent cricketing figures in the first half of the last century. Mynn, who was over 6 feet tall and weighed nearly 20 stone, was one of the outstanding players in the history of the game, remarkable both for his skill and personality.

89. *Cricket at Moulsey Hurst*, c. 1790.
Generally, but possibly mistakenly,
attributed to Richard Wilson, the
landscape painter.

the same man but once: if their lordships ever sold at all, you would peach upon them if ever after they dared to win. You'll try me once, and then you'll have me in a line like him of the mill last year.' No, sir, a man was a slave when once he sold to these folk: 'fool and knave aye go together.' Still, they found fools enough for their purpose; but rogues can never trust each other. One day, a sad quarrel arose between two of them, which opened the gentlemen's eyes too wide to close again to those practices. Two very big rogues at Lord's fell a quarrelling, and blows were given; a crowd drew round, and the gentlemen ordered them both into the pavilion. When the one began, 'You had 10*l.* to lose the Kent match, bowling leg long hops and missing catches.' 'And you were paid to lose at Swaffham.' – 'Why did that game with Surrey turn about – three runs to get, and you didn't make them?' Angry words come out fast; and, when they are circumstantial and square with previous suspicions, they are proofs as strong as holy writ. In one single-wicket match,' he continued, – 'and those were always great matches for the sporting men, because usually you had first-rate men on each side, and their merits known, – dishonesty was as plain as this: just as a player was coming in, (John B. will confess this if you talk of the match,) he said to me, 'You'll let me score five or six, for appearances, won't you, for I am not going to make many if I can?' 'Yes,' I said, 'you

rogue, you shall if I can *not* help it.' – But, when a game was all but won, and the odds heavy, and all one way, it was cruel to see how the fortune of the day then would change about. In that Kent match, – you can turn to it in your book (Bentley's scores), played 28th July, 1807, on Penenden Heath, – I and Lord Frederick had scored sixty-one, and thirty remained to win, and six of the best men in England went out for eleven runs. Well, sir, I lost some money by that match, and as seven of us were walking homewards to meet a coach, a gentleman who had backed the match drove by and said, 'Jump up, my boys, we have all lost together. I need not mind if I hire a pair of horses extra next town, for I have lost money enough to pay for twenty pair or more.' Well, thought I, as I rode along, you have rogues enough in your carriage now, sir, if the truth were told, I'll answer for it; and, one of them let out the secret, some ten years after. But, sir, I can't help laughing when I tell you: once, there was a single-wicket match played at Lord's, and a man on each side was paid to lose. One was bowler, and the other batsman, when the game came to a near point. I knew their politics, the rascals, and saw in a minute how things stood; and how I did laugh to be sure. For seven balls together, one would not bowl straight, and the other would not hit; but at last a straight ball must come, and down went the wicket.'

From other information received, I could tell this veteran that, even in his much-repented Nottingham match, his was not the only side that had men resolved to lose. The match was sold for Nottingham too, and that with less success, for Nottingham won: an event the less difficult to accomplish, as Lord Frederick Beauclerk broke a finger in an attempt to stop an angry and furious throw from Shearman, whom he had scolded for slack play. His Lordship batted with one hand. Afterwards lock-jaw threatened; and Lord Frederick was, well nigh, a victim to Cricket!

It is true, Clarke, who played in the match, thought all was fair: still, he admits, he heard one Nottingham man accused, on the field, by his own side of foul play. This confirms the evidence of the Rev. C. W., no slight authority in Nottingham matches, who said he was cautioned before the match that all would not be fair.

'This practice of selling matches,' said Beldham, 'produced strange things sometimes. Once, I remember, England was playing Surrey, and, in my judgment, Surrey had the best side; still I found the Legs were betting seven to four against Surrey! This time, they were done; for they betted on the belief that some Surrey men had sold the match: but, Surrey then played to win.'

'Crockford used to be seen about Lord's, and Mr. Gully also occasionally; but, only for the society of sporting men: they did not understand the game, and I never saw them bet. Mr. Gully was often talking to me about the game for one season; but,' said the old man, as he smoothed down his smockfrock, with all the confidence in the world, 'I could never put any sense into him! He knew plenty about fighting, and afterwards of horse-racing; but a man cannot learn the odds of cricket unless he is something of a player.'

CRICKET MATCH BETWEEN TWENTY-TWO FEMALES

From *Sporting Anecdotes* by Pierce Egan, 1820

In the year 1811, on Wednesday, the 2nd of October, in a field belonging to Mr. Strong, at the back of Newington-green, near Hall's pond, Middlesex, this singular performance between the Hampshire and Surrey heroines, commenced at eleven o'clock in the morning. It was made by two noblemen, for five hundred guineas a-side. The performers in this contest were of all ages and sizes, from *fourteen* to *sixty*; the young had shawls, and the old long cloaks. The Hampshire were distinguished by the colour of *true blue*, which was pinned in their bonnets, in the shape of the Prince's plume. The Surrey were equally smart; their colours were *blue*, surmounted with *orange*. The latter *eleven* consisted of Ann Baker (sixty years of age, the best runner and bowler on that side), Ann Taylor, Maria Barfatt, Hannah Higgs, Elizabeth Gale, Hannah Collas, Hannah Bartlett, Maria Cooke, Charlotte Cooke, Elizabeth Stock, and Mary Fry.

The Hampshire eleven were Sarah Luff, Charlotte Pulain, Hannah Parker, Elizabeth Smith, Martha Smith, Mary Woodson, Nancy Porter, Ann Poulters, Mary Novell, Mary Hislock, and Mary Jougan.

Very excellent play took place; one of the Hampshire lasses made forty-one innings before she was thrown out; and, at the conclusion of the day's sport, the Hampshire eleven were 81 ahead – the unfavourableness of the weather prevented any more sport that day, though the ground was filled with spectators. On the following day, the Surrey lasses kept the field with great success; and on Monday, the 7th, being the last day to decide the contest, an unusual assemblage of elegant persons were on the ground. At three o'clock the match was won by the Hampshire lasses, who not being willing to leave the field at so early an hour, and having only won by two innings, they played a single game, in which they were also successful. Afterwards they marched in triumph to the Angel, at Islington, where a handsome entertainment had been provided for them by the Nobleman that made the match.

SINGULAR CRICKET MATCHES
AND RACES BETWEEN ELEVEN MEN WITH ONE LEG AGAINST THE SAME NUMBER WITH ONE ARM – ALL GREENWICH PENSIONERS

From *Sporting Anecdotes* by Pierce Egan, 1820

From the novelty of an advertisement announcing a cricket-match to be played by *eleven Greenwich pensioners with one leg against eleven with one arm*, for one thousand guineas, at the new Cricket-Ground, Montpelier-Gardens, Walworth, in 1796, an immense concourse of people assembled. About nine o'clock the men arrived in Three Greenwich stages; about ten the wickets were pitched, and the match commenced. Those with but one leg had the first innings, a scene of riot and confusion took place, owing to the pressure of the populace to gain admittance: the gates were forced open, parts of the fencing broke down, and a great

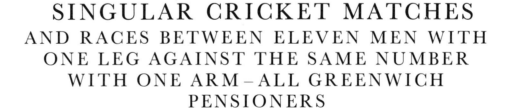

90. *Above* Cricket at Lords in 1822, published in 1894. Lords Ground, home of the Marylebone Cricket Club, was opened in 1809, but it did not gain its present popularity until 1877, when Middlesex began to use it as their home ground. The match pictured here is probably an imaginary one.

91. *Left Rural sports, or a cricket match extraordinary,* by Thomas Rowlandson, 1811. The match between 11 Hampshire women and 11 women from Surrey which took place on Wednesday, October 3rd, 1811.

ALFRED MYNN

William Jeffrey Prowse, c.1758

Jackson's pace is very fearful, Willsher's hand is very high;
William Caffyn has good judgment, and an admirable eye;
Jemmy Grundy's cool and clever, almost always on the spot;
Tinsley's slows are often telling, though they sometimes catch it hot.
But however good their trundling, pitch or pace, or break or spin,
Still the monarch of all bowlers, to my mind, was Alfred Mynn.

Richard Daft is cool and cautious, with his safe and graceful play;
If George Griffith gets a loose one he will send it far away;
You may bowl your best at Hayward, and whatever style you try
Will be vanquished by the master's steady hand and certain eye.
But whatever fame and glory these and other bats may win.
Still the monarch of hard hitters, to my mind, was Alfred Mynn.

With his tall and stately presence, with his nobly moulded form,
His broad hand was ever open, his brave heart was ever warm;
All were proud of him, all loved him. As the changing seasons pass,
As our champion lies a-sleeping underneath yon Kentish grass,
Proudly, sadly, we will name him; to forget him were a sin;
Lightly lie the turf upon thee, kind and manly Alfred Mynn!

JOHN SMALL (1737-1826)

Pierce Egan (1772-1849)

Here lies, bowled out by Death's unerring ball,
A Cricketer renowned, by name John Small.
But though his name was Small, yet great his fame,
For nobly did he play the noble game;
His life was like his innings, long and good,
Full ninety summers he had death withstood.
At length the ninetieth winter came, when (fate
Not leaving him one solitary mate)
This last of Hambledonians, old John Small,
Gave up his bat and ball, his leather, wax and all.

number of persons having got upon the top of a stable, the roof broke in, and many were taken out much bruised. About six o'clock the game was renewed, and those with one arm got but forty-two runs during their innings. The one legs commenced their second innings, and six were bowled out after they got sixty runs, so that they left off one hundred and eleven more than those with one arm.

The match was played again on the Wednesday following, and the men with *one leg* beat the *one arms* by one hundred and three runnings. After the match was finished, the eleven *one-legged* men ran one hundred yards for twenty guineas. The three first divided the money.

92. English lady cricketers in action, by Lucien Davies, from the *Illustrated London News*, 1890.

FENCING

BACKSWORDSMANSHIP

From *A Treatise Upon The Useful Science of Defence* by Capt. John Godfrey, 1747

Before I enter upon the Characters of the most eminent Masters, who have come within my Observation, I must take notice of the Superiority the Back-Sword has over the Small, in point of Use. Indeed as we cannot put a Stop to the natural Passions of Mankind, which, according to their Constitution and Temperament, more or less excite them to Mischief, if not proportionably checked by Reason; we must endeavour at the readiest Means of putting it out of their power to do us that Mischief their Passions prompt them to. It is therefore requisite to learn the Small-Sword, in order to guard against the Attempts of that Man, with whose brutal Ferocity no Reason will prevail: But then that Necessity is productive of Pain and Misery, though it tends to the Preservation of your Life. Killing a Man, when you are forced upon the Defensive, clears you in human Laws; but how far you are justified in Christianity, the Gospel best can tell you. There is a Consciousness attends all Actions, which is the strongest Monitor; and that Consciousness will not leave a Man undisturbed after his Fellow-Creature is laid bleeding at his Feet, though from the highest Provocation, and in his necessary self-defence. But Laws divine as well as human justify and protect you in your Country's Cause. Sure the wide Difference between killing numbers of your Enemy in Battle, and one Man in a Quarrel, ever so much in your own Defence, every calm thinking Man cannot but allow.

It is therefore that the Small-Sword, in point of true Reason, is not necessary; it is only a subservient Instrument to our Passions. This is viewing it in the tenderest Light; but I fear it oftener proves, proportionably to its Practice, an Incentive and Encouragement to Mischief.

But the Back-Sword, sure, must be distinguished from the other, because it is as necessary in the Army, as the other is mischievous in Quarrels, and deadly in Duels. The Small-Sword is the Call of Honour, the Back-Sword the Call of Duty. I wish Honour had more Acquaintance with Honesty than it generally has. There is a Kind of Honour,

which will carry a Man behind Montague House with another, when it will not pay his Debts, though he has the wherewithal to do it. True Honour must be very intimate with Honesty, and I will venture to affirm that, where the latter is not, the former has but a mean existence. It need not be said I here discourage the Small-Sword, I only oppose its Abuse; I own, I have preached a little, but I think what I have advanced is true Doctrine: But as few of us can arrive to that prodigious Meekness, it is necessary to be Masters of our Sword, to guard against those Passions we cannot put a Stop to. I am not that Saint to advise a Man to let another pull him by the Nose; but then I would have him to be the brave User of his Sword, and not the quarrelsome. Quarrelsomeness and Bravery, I take to be Strangers, and the more Bravery I have found in a Man, I have always observed in him the more Unwillingness to Quarrel. I yet highly recommend the Small-Sword teaching, if it were only (as I have before hinted) to introduce you better, and

93. Mr. H. Angelo's Fencing Academy, by Thomas Rowlandson, 1791.

establish you stronger in the Back-Sword. The Back-Sword must be allowed essentially necessary among the Horse; and I could wish it were more practised, than I find it is. Sure it ought to be a Part of a Trooper's Duty to learn the Back-Sword, as much as of the Foot to learn the common Exercise; and the Exercise of the former's Sword ought to be urged, as much as that of the latter's Firelock. If a Troop of FIGS were engaged with a Troop of Men, ignorant of the Back-Sword, I would ask, which has the better chance? I believe it will be granted, that a considerable superior Strength in the latter would not be an equivalent Advantage to the Skill and Judgement of the former.

We are allowed to be more expert in the Back-Sword than any other Nation, and it would be a pity, if we were not to continue so. In FIGG'S Time, the Spirit of it was greatly kept up; but I have been often sorry to find it dwindle, and in a Manner, die away with him. It must be allowed that those amphitheatrical Practices were productive of some ill, as they gave some Encouragement to Idleness and Extravagance among the Vulgar. But there is hardly any good useful Thing, but what leaves an opening for Mischief, and which is not liable to Abuse. Those Practices are certainly highly necessary, and the Encouragement of Back-Sword Fighting, and Boxing, I think Commendable; the former for the Uses which have been mentioned; the latter, and both; to feed and keep up the British Spirit. Courage I allow to be chiefly natural, probably owing to the Complexion and Constitution of our Bodies, and flowing in the different Texture of the Blood and juices; but sure it is, in a great measure, acquired by Use, and Familiarity with Danger. Emulation and the love of Glory are great Breeders of it. To what Pitch of daring do we not see them carry Men? And how observable is it in Miniature among the Boys, who, almost as soon as they can go alone, get into their Postures, and bear their little bloody Noses, rather than be stigmatised for Cowards?

CHARACTERS OF THE MASTERS

TIMOTHY BUCK was a most solid Master, it was apparent in his Performances, even when grown decrepid, and his old Age could not hide his uncommon Judgement. He was the Pillar of the Art, and all his Followers, who excelled, built upon him.

MR. MILLAR was the palpable Gentleman though the Prize-Fighter. He was a most beautiful Picture on the Stage, taking in all his Attitudes, and vastly engaging in his Demeanor. There was such an easy Action in

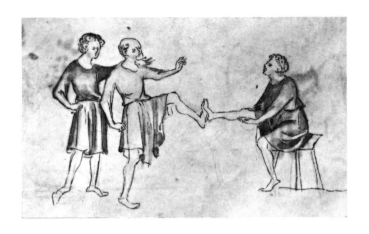

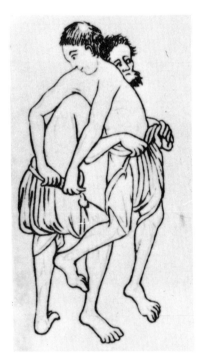

94. *Top* Foot-wrestling, from a 14th-century manuscript.

95. *Above* Wrestling, a drawing after an illumination in the *Luttrell Psalter*, c. 1340.

96. *Right The Laws of the Game of Dutch-pins* by W. Olive, engraved by J. Royce and published in 1787.

him, unconcerned Behaviour and agreeable Smile in the midst of Fighting, that one could not help being prejudiced in his Favour.

FIGG was the Atlas of the Sword, and may he remain the gladiating Statue! In him, Strength, Resolution, and unparallel'd Judgement conspired to form a matchless Master. There was a Majesty shone in his Countenance, and blazed in all his Actions, beyond all I ever saw. His right Leg bold and firm, and his left which could hardly ever be disturbed, gave him the surprising Advantage already proved, and struck his Adversary with Despair and Panic. He had that peculiar way of stepping in, I spoke of, in a *Parry*; he knew his arm and its just time of moving, just as much a greater MASTER, than any other I ever saw, as he was a greater Judge of *Time* and *Measure*.

WILLIAM GILL was a Swords-Man formed by FIGG's own Hand, and by his Example turned out a complete Piece of Work. I never beheld any Body better for the Leg than GILL. His Excellence lay in doing it from the *Inside*; and I hardly ever knew him attempt it from the *Outside*. From the narrow Way he had of going down, (which was mostly without receiving) he oftener hit the Leg than any one; and from the drawing Stroke, caused by that sweeping Turn of the Wrist, and his proper way of holding his Sword, his Cuts were remarkably more severe and deep. I never was an Eye-Witness to such a Cut in the Leg, as he gave one BUTLER, an Irishman, a bold resolute Man, but an awkward Swords-Man. His Leg was laid quite open, his Calf falling down to his Ancle. It was soon stitched up; but from the Ignorance of a Surgeon adapted to his mean Circumstances, it mortified; Mr. *Cheselden* was applied to for amputation, but too late for his true Judgement to interfere in. He immediately perceived the Mortification to forbid his Skill; and refused to be concerned in what he knew to be beyond his Power. But another noted one was applied to, who, through less Judgement, or Value for his Character, cut off his Leg above the Knee, but the Mortification had got the Start of his Instruments, and BUTLER soon expired.

CONCERNING THE HUNGERFORD REVEL, ETC.

From *The Everyday Book* by William Hone. Vol. II, 1826

Sir, – Your correspondent C.T.p.1207, having given a description of 'Purton Fair', my grandmother and father born there, the birth-place of Anne Boleyn, I feel interested in the spot of my progenitors. C.T., speaking of old 'Corey Dyne,' the gipsy, says a man named *Blackford* was the most noted Backsword-player of his day. He bore off the prizes then played for in London, Bath, Bristol, and Gloucester. When very young, at Lyneham Grammar-School, I recollect this frontispiece despoiler broke fourteen heads, one after another; in the fifteenth bout,

97. *Above* Brook Green Fair, by Thomas Rowlandson, 1771.

98. *Left* Tenterden Park races, drawn and engraved by R. Cruikshank, from *Finish to the Adventures of Tom, Jerry and Logic* by Pierce Egan, 1828. The winner's prizes, which are hanging from the lamp-post in the centre, were a leg of mutton and a lady's shift.

however, he pretty nearly found his match in the person of Isaac Bushel, a blacksmith of this place, who could bite a nail asunder, eat a shoulder of mutton with appendages, or fight friend or foe for love or money. It was a saying, 'Bushel could take enough to kill a dozen men,' nor was his head unlike his name: he was the village Wat Tyler.

When the Somerset youths played with the Wiltshire on a stage on Calne-green, two years since, one of Blackford's descendants gave a feeling proof of head-breaking with other heads of this blood-letting art, in which stratagem is used to conceal the crimson gush chiefly by sucking. Like fencing, attitude and agility are the great assistants to ensure success in backsword-playing; the basket is also of great service to the receiving of blows, and protecting the muscles of the wrist. The greatest exploits remembered at Purton by the present memorialist, arose out of the 'Coronation of George the Third.' All the festivities of the seasons were concentrated, and May games and Christmas customs, without regard to usage, in full exercise. The belfry was filled day after day; any one that could pull a rope might ring, which is no easy task; the bells are deep, and two or three men usually raise the tenor. Some of the Blackfords lie in Purton churchyard.

October 5. *,*,P.

October 20, 1826.

Dear Sir, – In your last week's number of the *Every-Day Book*, your correspondent *,*,P. gives a short account of Blackford, the backsword-player, and also mentions one of his descendants who signalized himself at the 'Hungerford revel' about two years since. In the year 1820, I visited the latter revel; perhaps a description may be acceptable to you, and amusing to your readers.

I think it may be generally allowed that Wiltshire, and the western counties, keep up their primitive customs more than any counties. This is greatly to the credit of the inhabitants; for these usages tend to promote cheerful intercourse and friendly feeling among the residents in the different villages, who on such occasions assemble together. In Wiltshire I have remarked various customs, particularly at Christmas, which I have never seen or heard of in any other place. If these customs were witnessed by a stranger, I am sure he must fancy the good old days of yore, where every season brought its particular custom, which was always strictly adhered to.

Wiltshire consists of beautiful and extensive downs, and rich meadow and pasture lands, which support some of the finest dairies and farms that can be met with in the kingdom. The natives are a very strong and hardy set of men, and are particularly fond of robust sports; their chief and favourite amusement is back-swording, or singlestick, for which they are as greatly celebrated as the inhabitants of the adjoining counties, Somersetshire and Gloucestershire.

At this game there are several rules observed. They play with a large round stick, which must be three feet long, with a basket prefixed to one end as a guard for the hand. The combatants throw off their hats and

9. THE CUTTER YACHT VOLANTE, 48 TONS, R.T.Y.C.

From a print after T. S. Robbins, engraved by E. T. Dolby, and published by Messrs. Fores, London, June 8th, 1852. 17½ins × 12ins

The cutter Volante, owned by John L. Craigie, was a well-known and successful racing yacht during her relatively short life. She was built by Harvey and Sons in 1851, and wrecked on September 12th 1869, when she dragged her anchor and ran on to Ryde Sands. The Royal Thames Yacht Club, of which Mr Craigie was a member, was founded in 1823, and is still flourishing. In the year Volante was built, she was one of a group of seventeen of the best yachts of the Royal Yacht Squadron, and on August 22nd of 1851 took part in the historic race round the Isle of Wight against the visiting schooner America, of 170 tons, owned by several members of the New York Yacht Club. The prize was a cup worth £100 given by the Royal Yacht Squadron, and to the surprise of English yachtsmen, America won it easily. In 1857 the cup was presented to the New York Yacht Club, and since then has been known as the America's Cup. In spite of the efforts of Sir Thomas Lipton, Sopwith and others, it has never been won back. Volante was unlucky in the 1851 race – she collided with the yacht Freak and had to retire.

Volante is pictured here winning the Grand Challenge Cup on May 14th, 1852. This cup, valued at 200 guineas, was presented by the Royal Thames Yacht Club, and was one of the major events of their yachting calendar.

99. *Above* Duck-hunting, by Samuel Alken, engraved by Percy Roberts and published in 1823.

100. *Right* A 19th-century caricature of dancing.

THE CUTTER YACHT "VOLANTE"

upper garments, with the exception of the shirt, and have the left hand tied to the side, so that they cannot defend themselves with that hand. They brandish the stick over the head, guarding off the adversary's blows, and striking him whenever the opportunity occurs. Great skill is often used in the defence. I have seen two men play for upwards of half an hour without once hitting each other. The blood must flow an inch from some part of the head, before either party is declared victor.

Blackford, the backsword player, was a butcher residing at Swindon; he died a few years ago. His 'successor' is a blacksmith at Lyddington, named Morris Pope, who is considered the best player of the day, and generally carries off the prizes at the Hungerford revel, which he always attends. This revel is attended by all the best players in Wiltshire and Somersetshire, between whom the contest lies. To commence the fray, twenty very excellent players are selected from each county; the contest lasts a considerable time, and is always severe, but the Wiltshire men are generally conquerors. Their principal characteristics are skill, strength, and courage – this is generally allowed by all who are acquainted with them.

But Hungerford revel is not a scene of contention alone, it consists of all kinds of rustic sports, which afford capital fun to the spectators. They may be laid out thus –

1st. *Girls running for 'smocks'*, etc., which is a well-known amusement at country fairs.

2d. *Climbing the greasy pole* for a piece of bacon which is placed on the top. This affords very great amusement, as it is a difficult thing to be accomplished. The climber, perhaps, may get near the top of the pole, and has it in his power to hold himself up by both hands, but the moment he raises one hand to unhook the prize, he is almost sure to slide down again with great rapidity, bearing all below him who are so foolish as to climb after him.

3d. *Old women drinking hot tea for snuff*. Whoever can drink it the quickest and hottest gains the prize.

4th. *Grinning through horse-collars*. Several Hodges stand in a row, each holding a collar; whoever can make the ugliest face through it gains the prize. This feat is also performed by old women, and certainly the latter are the most amusing.

5th. *Racing between twenty and thirty old women for a pound of tea*. This occasions much merriment, and it is sometimes astonishing to see with

101. *Left* Donkey racing: an 18th-century woodcut.

102. *Above* A game of skittles: an early 19th-century woodcut.

FOOTBALL

A DISPENSATION

Dispensation granted from Avignon by Pope John XXII 1321

To William de Spalding, canon of Scoldham, of the order of Sempringham. During the game at ball as he kicked the ball, a lay friend of his, also called William, ran against him and wounded himself on a sheathed knife carried by the canon, so severely that he died within six days. Dispensation is granted, as no blame is attached to William de Spalding, who, feeling deeply the death of his friend, and fearing what might be said by his enemies, has applied to the pope.

THOSE AGAINST

Thomas Elyot, 1531

BEASTLIE FURIE

Footeballe, wherein is nothinge but beastlie furie and extreme violence, whereof procedeth hurte and consequently rancour, and malice do remaine with them that be wounded; wherefore it is to be put in perpetuall silence.

107. *Above Football in Crowe Street*, 1721.

108. *Right* A detail from the 14th-century misericorde in Gloucester Cathedral, depicting an early form of football.

COVENT GARDEN

John Gay, 1716

Where Covent Garden's famous Temple stands,
That boasts the work of Jones' immortal Hands,
Columns, with plain Magnificence, appear,
And graceful Porches lead around the Squares:
Here oft my Course I bend, when lo! from far
I spy the furies of the Foot-ball War:
The Prentice quits his Shop, to join the Crew,
Increasing Crowds the flying Game pursue.
Thus, as you roll the Ball o'er snowy Ground,
The gath'ring Globe augments with ev'ry Round.
But whither shall I run? The Throng draws nigh,
The Ball now skims the street, now soars on high;
The dex'trous Glazier strong returns the Bound,
And gingling Sashes on the Pent-house sound.

ECHE TIME AND SEASON

Alexander Barclay, 1514

Eche time and season hath his delite & joyes,
Loke in the stretes, beholde the little boyes,
Howe in fruit season for joy they sing and hop,
In Lent in eche one full busy with his top
And nowe in winter for all the grevous cold,
All rent and ragged a man may them beholde,
They have great pleasour supposing well to dine,
When men be busied in killing of fat swine,
They get the bladder and blow it great and thin,
With many beanes or peason put within;
It ratleth, soundeth, and shineth clere & feyre,
While it is throwen and caste up in the ayre.
Eche one contendeth and hath a great delite
With foote & hande the bladder for to smite:
If it fall to grounde they lifte it up agayne,
This wise to labour they count it for no paine,
Renning and leaping they drive away the colde.
The sturdie plowman, lustie, strong, & bolde
Overcommeth the winter with driving the footeball,
Forgetting labour and many a grevous fall.

GOWNBOYS *v* REST OF SCHOOL

From *Charterhouse Old and New* by Wilmot and Smeatfield, 1892

The cloister, a species of tunnel paved with smooth flag-stones, but roughly constructed with sharp, jagged flints at its sides, was about 70 yards long, 9 feet wide, and 12 feet high. It was supported by horizontal iron bars, and had a number of buttresses facing outwards on to Upper Green, with large square windows. In the middle it opened out east and west, and formed a little square called Middle Briers. The whole cloister extended from Gownboys to the Gownboy Dining Hall. At the north end there was a narrow entrance leading into Gownboys; at the South, a small door leading out on to the Green. On Wednesday afternoons a written notice, 'All Fags to be in Cloisters at 2.30', used to be posted up on the principal archway. Say that the match was to be between Gownboys v. Rest of School. At the appointed time the Fags would assemble, and take up their position twenty strong at each end of Cloisters; the Gownboy Fags, at the door leading to their own House; the Rest-of-School Fags, at the South door leading on to Green. The boys of the higher forms would then range themselves down the Cloisters, the football being started from Middle Briers. As may naturally be supposed, the ball very soon got into one of the buttresses, when a terrific squash would be the result, some fifty or sixty boys huddled together, vigorously

'roughing', kicking, and shoving to extricate the ball. A skilful player, feeling that he had the ball in front of his legs, would patiently bide his time, until, perceiving an opportunity, he would dexterously work out the ball and rush wildly with it down Cloisters towards the coveted goal. The squash would then dissolve and go in pursuit. Now was the time for the pluck and judgement of the Fags to be tried. To prevent the ball getting in amongst them at the goal, one of the foremost Fags would rush out and engage the onset of the dribbling foe, generally to be sent spinning head over heels for five yards along the stones. It served a purpose, however, for it not only gave his side time to come up, but also his fellow Fags encouragement to show a close and firm front. If the boy with the ball happened to be well backed up by his own Houses, they

109. *Top left* Football: an early 19th-century caricature by H. Heath.

110. *Above* Football at Rugby College, where Rugby football originated when one of the pupils, William Webb Ellis, in 1823 'first took the ball into his arms and ran'. By W. Thomas, 1870.

of triumph and encouragement during the performance beggar all description.

In less than six minutes and a half all but one solitary rat was destroyed, and this the hero of the corn-bin finished. He then retired, with scarcely a scratch, amid the acclamations of his friends. A battle royal of seven cocks followed, for a flitch of bacon, which was '*brought to a wrangle*,' and settled by a division of the prize. The *glims* were then dowsed, and a prime lark ensued, by way of *finale*, which produced *claret* and a few *queer ogles*.

JUSTICE HIGDEN, A GAMESTER

From *Lives of the Gamesters* by Theophilus Lucas, 1714

This comical spark was also a great gamester, especially at dice; and one night he and another of his fraternity going to a gaming-house, Higden draws a chair and sits down, but as often as the box came to him, he past it, and sat only as a spectator; till at last one of those who were at play said to him in a pet, Sir, if you won't play, what do you sit there for? Upon which he snatch'd up the box, and said, Set me what you will, and I'll throw at it. One of the gentlemen set him 2 guineas, which he won, and then he set him 4, which he nick'd also; the rest of the gentlemen who were at the table took his part who had lost, and set to Higden, who by some art, and some luck, won 120 guineas; and presently after his companion by the fire-side, who ask'd him how he durst be so audacious as to venture at first to play, knowing he had not a shilling in his pocket. One of the losers over-hearing what was said, How's that, quoth he, had you no money when you began to play? That's no matter, reply'd Higden, I have enough now; and if you had won of me, you must have contented to have kick'd, buffeted or pump'd me, and you should have done it so long till you said you was satisfy'd. Besides, Sir, I am a soldier, and have often faced the mouths of thundring canons for 8 shillings a day, and do you think I would not hazard the tossing in a blanket for the money I have won to night. All that were concern'd wonder'd at his confidence; but he laugh'd heartily at their folly, and his own good fortune; and so march'd off with a light heart, and a heavy purse. Afterwards, to make himself as miserable as he could, he turn'd poet, when going into Ireland, he writ there a play or two, and shortly after dy'd there very poor, in 1703, aged 44.

DEEP PLAY

From *Sporting Anecdotes* by Pierce Egan, 1820

The late General Ogle was a noble-minded man, a pleasant companion, a sincere friend, and a most indulgent parent. His only failing – which in these fashionable times, perhaps, will not be called a fault – was his unconquerable attachment to play.

A few weeks before he was to sail for India, he constantly attended Pain's, in Charles-street, St. James's Square, where he alternately won and lost large sums. One evening there were before him two wooden bowls full of gold, which held fifteen hundred guineas each: and also four thousand guineas in *rouleaus* which he had won. – When the box came to him, he shook the dice, and with great coolness and pleasantry said – 'Come, I'll either win or lose seven thousand upon this hand: will any gentleman set me the whole? Seven thousand is the main.' Then, rattling the dice once more, cast the box from him and quitted it, the dice remaining covered. Though the general did not consider this too large a sum for one man to risk at a single throw, the rest of the company did, and for some time he remained unset. He then said – 'Well, gentlemen, will you make it up amongst you?' One set him £500, another £500. – 'Come,' says he, 'whilst you are making up this money – £7000,

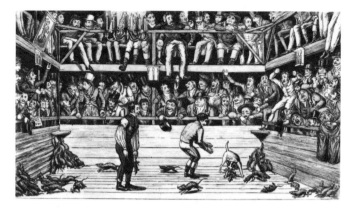

112. *Above* Billy the celebrated ratter, from *Anecdotes of the Turf, the Chase, the Ring and the Stage* by Pierce Egan, 1827. Billy had achieved the record, in August 1823, of killing 100 rats in 12 minutes.

113. *Left Betting Post* by Thomas Rowlandson, 1801.

114. *A Match against Time, or Wood beats Blood and Bone*, published in 1819.

I'll tell you a story.' Here he began to relate a story, that was pertinent to the moment; but perceiving that he was completely set, stopped short – laid his hand upon the box, saying, 'I believe I am set, gentlemen?' – 'Yes, sir: seven is the main.' He threw out! then, with astonishing coolness, took up his snuff-box, and smiling, exclaimed, 'Now, gentlemen, I'll finish my story, if you please!'

THIMBLE AND PEA

From *The Everyday Book* by William Hone. Vol. I, June 8th, 1825

On the 8th of June, 1825, a publican in the neighbourhood of Whitechapel was charged at the Public Office, Bow-street, by Mr. John Francis Panchaud, a foreigner, with having, in conjunction with several other persons, defrauded him of a 10*l.* note, at Ascot Heath race-course, on the Thursday preceding. The alleged fraud, or robbery, was effected by means of an unfair game known among the frequenters of races and fairs by the name of 'the thimble rig,' of which J. Smith, the officer, this day gave the following description to Mr. Minshull, in order that the worthy magistrate might perfectly understand the case:– A gang of seven or eight, or more, set up a table, but they all appear strangers to each other, and unconnected with the game, except one who conducts it, and who appears to be the sole proprietor. This master of the ceremonies has three thimbles, and is provided with a number of peas, or pepper-corns. He puts one under each thimble, or perhaps only under one or two, as the case may be. He then offers a bet as to which thimble a pepper-corn is or is not under, and offers at first such a wager as is eagerly taken by those round the table, and he loses. He pays the losings freely, and the other members of this joint-stock company affect to laugh at him, as what they call a 'good flat.' Having thus drawn the attention, and probably excited the cupidity of a stranger, who appears to have money, they suffer him to win a stake or two, and get him to increase his bets. When he seems thoroughly in the humour, the master of the table lifts a thimble, under which is a pepper-corn, and turning his head aside to speak to some one, he suffers the corn to roll off; and, seeming to be unconscious of this, he replaces the thimble, and offers bets to any amount that there is a corn underneath that particular thimble. The stranger having seen the corn roll off 'with his own eyes,' as the phrase is, chuckles to himself, and eagerly takes the bet; the thimble is removed, and behold! – there is a pepper-corn under it still, the fellow having dexterously slipped another under it when the first

rolled off the table. 'So that the plain fact is, sir,' continued Smith, 'that the stranger, fancying he is taking in the master of the table, cheerfully stakes his money with a dead certainty, as he supposes, of winning, and he finds that he has been taken in himself.' Smith said, he had known instances of gentlemen getting from their carriages, and in a few moments ridding themselves of 20*l.* or 30*l.*, or perhaps more, and going off wondering at their folly, and looking uncommon silly.

It appeared that Mr. Panchaud went up to one of these tables, at which the defendant and many others were playing, and after winning two or three times, the trick above described was commenced. The conductor of the game offered a bet of 5*l.*, and Mr. Panchaud having seen the pepper-corn roll off, took the wager, and put down a 10*l.* note. In a moment after there was a general hustling, the table was upset, and the whole party speedily disappeared, together with the 10*l.* note. When the bet was offered, the defendant, who stood next to him, jogged his elbow, and said eagerly, 'Bet him, bet him; you must win, the ball is under our feet.' Mr. Panchaud had no doubt, from his whole manner, that the defendant was concerned with the others in the trick. The case stood over for further investigation. It is only mentioned here for the purpose of showing a species of slight of hand continued in our times to defraud the unwary.

STOOL-BALL

Robert Herrick (1591-1674)

At Stool-ball, Lucia, let us play,
   For Sugar-cakes and Wine;
Or for a Tansie let us pay,
   The losse or thine, or mine.

If thou, my Deere, a winner be
   At trundling of the Ball,
The wager thou shalt have, and me,
   And my misfortunes all.

But if (my Sweetest) I shall get,
   Then I desire but this:
That likewise I may pay the Bet,
   And have all for a kisse.

CURIOUS WAGER –
WALKING AGAINST EATING

From *Sporting Anecdotes* by Pierce Egan, 1820

This sporting event was decided at a public-house, at Knightsbridge: one Boyne, a labouring gardener, undertook, for the trifling sum of half a crown, to eat, without drinking, 24 red herrings and two ounces of mustard, while the landlord, a corpulent man, walked half a mile on the road. The pedestrian performed his march in somewhat less than nine minutes; but the hero of the jaw-bone had, in less than eight minutes, completed his task, and awaited the arrival of his opponent with a full pot, the first fruits of his victory.

GOFF

From *The Sports and Pastimes of the People of England* by Joseph Strutt, 1801

Goff, according to the present modification of the game, is performed with a bat not much unlike the bandy; the handle of this instrument is straight, and usually made of ash, about four feet and a half in length; the curvature is affixed to the bottom, faced with horn, and backed with lead; the ball is a little one, but exceedingly hard, being made with leather, and, as before observed, stuffed with feathers. There are generally two players, who have each of them his bat and ball. The game consists in driving the ball into certain holes made in the ground, which he who achieved the soonest, or in the fewest number of strokes, obtains the victory. The Goff lengths, or the spaces between the first and last holes, are sometimes extended to the distance of two or three miles; the number of intervening holes appears to be optional, but the balls must be struck into the holes, and not beyond them; when four persons play, two of them are sometimes partners, and have but one ball, which they strike alternately, but every man has his own bandy.

GOLF

From *Sporting Anecdotes* by Pierce Egan, 1820

Golf – There are many games played with a ball that require the assistance of a *club* or *bat*; and probably one of the most ancient among them, is the pastime now distinguished by the name of golf or goff. It is much practised in Scotland; is played there to great perfection, and a taste for it is kept up by the institution of societies for this special purpose. It is a diversion well calculated for exercising the body, and may always be taken in such moderation, as neither to overheat nor fatigue. It has in

115. Ladies playing golf at the Westward Ho! Golf Club at Bideford in 1873. The Westward Ho! course, home of the Royal North Devon Club, is the oldest course in England on its original site.

foolish risk of life and limb. But even the most ignorant can see what it is all about. Rackets and tennis, again, at once strike the beholder as being games which require great quickness of eye and great dexterity of hand. But there appears to be something singularly inane and foolish about a game of golf. Two middle-aged gentlemen strolling across a links followed by two boys staggering under the burden of a dozen

12. THE GOLFERS, SAINT ANDREWS, 1847

From a painting by C. Lees, RSA. 21⅜ins × 13¼ins

A match played at St. Andrews between Sir David Baird, Bart. and Sir Ralph Anstruther, Bart. on the one side, and Major Playfair and John Campbell, Esq., of Saddel, on the other. The scene is the 15th green on the Old Course. Major Playfair has just putted. His partner, Campbell of Saddel, calmer than the rest, is standing back to the right, behind the little girl with the refreshments, with his club over his shoulder. Baird, who always played in a tall hat, is the gentleman leaning forward watching the ball, with his club in his hand, and Anstruther, bareheaded, is the one with his foot near the hole, leaning back in an attitude of tension, as if he fears the putt will drop. All four were well-known players in their day, and members of the North Berwick Club as well as of the Royal and Ancient.

> 'There's Major Playfair, man of nerve unshaken,
> He knows a thing or two, or I'm mistaken.
> And, when he's pressed, can play a tearing game,
> He works for *certainty* and not for *Fame*;
> There's none – I'll back the assertion with a wager –
> Can play the heavy iron like the Major.'

Campbell was described by a contemporary writer as 'a sort of Magnus Apollo with the fashionables of his day. He was a great sporting man, and though a heavyweight rode remarkably well to hounds. He went in a balloon from Heriot's Hospital to Fife when such a thing was considered a bold feat. He was a noble-looking man, pompous in his manners, and very irascible.'

> 'Still Saddel walks, superb, improved in play
> Though his blue jacket now is turned to gray
> Still are his golf balls rife and clean as wont
> Still swears by Ammon and still bets the *blunt*
> Still plays all matches – still is often beat –
> And still, in iced punch, drowns each fresh defeat.'

Baird was another all-round sportsman, who listed his favourite occupations in the order of golf, salmon-fishing, deer-stalking and fox-hunting. Anstruther combined sport with political interests:

> 'Were he but once in Parliament, methinks
> And working *there* as well as on the *links*
> The burghs, I'll be bound, would not repent them
> That they had such a man to represent them.'

This being before the invention of golf-bags, the caddies carry the clubs in bundles under their arms. One wonders how a modern tournament player would feel about the green.

that respect the preference over cricket, tennis, or any other of those games which cannot be played without violence.

D———D SCOTCH CROQUET

From *Golf* by Horace G. Hutchinson, 1892

Since golf, when it has been once begun, exercises this fatal fascination upon its votaries, it is perhaps fortunate that of all games it appears to the uninitiated to be the most meaningless. A *melee* at football may appear to involve a perfectly unnecessary expenditure of energy and a

116. Members of the Royal Perth Golfing Society playing on the North Inch, by Macneill Macleay, 1842. The Perth Golfing Society was founded in 1824, and in 1833 was given the title 'Royal' by William IV – it was the first club to be honoured with this title.

THE GOLFERS
St ANDREWS
1847

queer-shaped implements, each player hitting along his own ball for no apparent object, in no obvious rivalry, and exercising in the process no obvious skill, do not make up a specially impressive picture to those who see it for the first time; and many are the curious theories advanced by the ignorant to explain the motives and actions of the players.

Two Englishmen, it is said, visited St. Andrews in the course of a Scotch tour. Looking out of the window of the train at the point where the railway runs along the links, they took their first survey of the game. The weather had been very wet, and at the bottom of some bunkers water was lying. 'These are the places,' said A to B, with ready ingenuity, 'where the Scotch play curling in winter.' 'No,' said B to A, 'there are the holes they use for golf, and the object of the player is to get out of one into another as quickly as he can manage it.' Armed with this superior knowledge, A proceeds down to the links, and finds an old gentleman struggling with destiny at the bottom of a bad bunker. At last the player succeeds in getting out his ball, but only with the result of sending it into the next bunker a few yards on. This is not an agreeable incident under any circumstances at golf; but conceive, if you can, the irritation of the player when he finds himself being loudly, and, as he no doubt thought, ironically congratulated by a spectator on the results of his stroke, and the well-merited success with which it had been rewarded! I do not know whether this story be apocryphal or not, but in any case the ignorance which it displays is not likely to be long continued in the southern portion of the island. There will soon be more greens in England than in Scotland, and more players of English extraction than of Scotch. 'Do you have much play here?' said someone to the keeper of a racket court in the neighbourhood of an English golf links. 'We used to, sir,' said the man; 'but ever since this d – d Scotch croquet has come into fashion, no one comes into the court.'

It is hard that a game which seems to those who do not play it to be so meaningless should be to those who do play it not only the most absorbing of existing games, but occasionally in the highest degree irritating to the nerves and to the temper. The fact itself will, I apprehend, hardly be denied, and the reason I suppose to be this, that as in most games action is rapid and more or less unpremeditated, failure seems less humiliating in itself, and there is less time to brood over it. In most games – e.g. cricket, tennis, football – effort succeeds effort in such quick succession that the memory of particular blunders is immediately effaced or deadened. There is leisure neither for self-examination nor for repentance. Even good resolutions scarce have time to form themselves, and as soon as one difficulty is surmounted, mind and body have

to brace themselves to meet the next. In the case of golf it is far otherwise. The player approaches his ball with every circumstance of mature deliberation. He meditates, or may meditate, for as long as he pleases on the precise method by which it may best be accomplished. No difficulties are made for him by his opponent; he has no obstacles to overcome but those which are material and inanimate. Is there not, then, some natural cause for irritation when, after every precaution has been taken to insure a drive of 150 or 180 yards, the unfortunate player sees his ball roll gently into the bottom of a bunker some twenty yards in front of the teeing ground and settle itself with every appearance of deliberate forethought at the bottom of the most inaccessible heel-mark therein? Such an event brings with it not merely disaster, but humiliation; and, as a last aggravation, the luckless performer has ample leisure to meditate over his mishap, to analyse its causes, to calculate the precise effects which it will have on the general fortunes of the day, and to divine the secret satisfaction with which his opponent has observed the difficulties

117. Golfing in the late 18th century.

in which he has so gratuitously involved himself. No wonder that persons of irritable nerves are occasionally goaded to fury. No wonder that the fury occasionally exhibits itself in violent and eccentric forms. Not, however, that the opponent is usually the object or victim of their wrath. He is too obviously guiltless of contributing to a 'foozle' to permit even an angry man to drag him into his quarrel with the laws of dynamics. It is true that he may have the most extraordinary and unmerited luck. According to my experience, opponents who are winning usually have. But still he can hardly be blamed because the man he is playing with 'tops' his ball or is 'short' with his putts. Let him only assume an aspect of colourless indifference or hypocritical sympathy, and the storm will in all probability not break over *him*.

Expletives more or less vigorous directed against himself, the ball, the club, the wind, the bunker, and the game, are therefore the most usual safety-valve for the fury of the disappointed golfer. But bad language is fortunately much gone out of use; and in any case the resources of profanity are not inexhaustible. Deeds, not words, are required in extreme cases to meet the exigencies of the situation; and, as justice, prudence, and politeness all conspire to shield his opponent from physical violence, it is on the clubs that under these circumstances vengeance most commonly descends. Most players content themselves with simply breaking the offending weapon against the ground. But some persons there are whose thirst for revenge cannot be satisfied by any such rapid or simple process. I have been told of one gentleman who threw the offending club upon the ground, and then with his niblick proceeded to punish it with piecemeal destruction, breaking its shaft into small pieces very much as criminals used to be broken upon the wheel. Even this procedure seemed inadequate to one infuriated golfer of whom I have heard. A shaft, be it broken into ever so many fragments, can be replaced and the implement be as good as new. Nothing less than destroying both head and shaft can insure its final disappearance from the world of golf. The club must not merely be broken, but must be destroyed, and from its hated remnants no new race must be permitted to arise for the torment and discomfiture of succeeding generations of golfers. This perfect consummation can, it is said, be attained by holding the club upright, the head resting on the ground, then placing one foot upon it and kicking it with the other, just at the point where head and shaft are bound together. By this simple expedient (which I respectfully commend to the attention of all short-tempered golfers) a 'root' and 'branch' policy may be effectually carried out by destroying at one stroke both the essential parts of the club.

If there are any who hold the opinion that measures such as this can never be justified by any series of golfing disasters, however aggravating, I would reply in the language of a gentleman who, when remonstrated with for using his clubs in one of the methods above described, responded with unanswerable logic, 'Is it not better to smash your dashed clubs than to lose your dashed temper?'

118. *Top* Hunting, from the *Queen Mary Psalter*, c. 1310.

119. *Above* Boar-hunting, from the *Queen Mary Psalter*, c. 1310.

120. *Right* Coursing, by W. J. Rayer, engraved by J. Harris, c. 1836.

HUNTING

AMONG THE HOUNDS

From *Joseph Andrews* by Henry Fielding, 1742

Joseph no sooner perceived the position of Adams, who was stretched on his back, and snored louder than the usual braying of the animal with long ears, than he turned towards Fanny, and, taking her by the hand, began a dalliance, which, tho' consistent with the purest innocence and decency, neither he would have attempted, nor she permitted, before any witness. Whilst they amused themselves in this harmless and delightful manner, they heard a pack of hounds approaching in full cry towards them, and presently afterwards saw a hare pop forth from the wood, and, crossing the water, land within a few yards of them in the meadows. The hare was no sooner on shore, than it seated itself on its hinder legs, and listened to the sound of the pursuers. Fanny was wonderfully pleased with the little wretch, and eagerly longed to have it in her arms that she might preserve it from the dangers which seemed to threaten it; but the rational part of the creation do not always aptly distinguish their friends from their foes; what wonder then if this silly creature the moment it beheld her, fled from the friend, who would have protected it, and, traversing the meadows again, passed the little rivulet on the opposite side. It was however so spent and weak, that it fell down twice or thrice in its way. This affected the tender heart of Fanny, who exclaimed, with tears in her eyes, against the barbarity of worrying a poor innocent defenceless animal out of its life, and putting it to the extremest torture for diversion. She had not much time to make reflections of this kind; for on a sudden the hounds rushed thro' the wood, which resounded with their throats and the throats of their retinue who attended them on horseback. The dogs now passed the rivulet, and pursued the footsteps of the hare; five horsemen attempted to leap over, three of whom succeeded, and two were in the attempt thrown from their saddles into the water; their companions, and their own horses too, proceeded after their sport, and left their friends and riders to invoke the assistance of fortune, or employ the more active means of strength and agility for their deliverance. Joseph however was not so

unconcerned on this occasion; he left Fanny for a moment to herself, and ran to the gentlemen, who were immediately on their legs, shaking their ears, and easily with the help of his hand attained the bank (for the rivulet was not at all deep); and without staying to thank their kind assister, ran dripping across the meadow, calling to their brother sportsmen to stop their horses: but they heard them not.

The hounds were now very little behind their poor reeling, staggering prey, which, fainting almost at every step, crawled through the wood, and had almost got round to the place where Fanny stood, when it was overtaken by its enemies; and, being driven out of the covert, was

121. *The Kill* by Thomas Rowlandson, 1787. One of a series of fox-hunting scenes depicting George IV (centre) when he was Prince of Wales.

122. Badger-hunting, 18th century. Surprisingly, badger-hunting was considered to be one of the most dangerous forms of hunting. Badgers can fight viciously when cornered, and it was not unusual for hounds to be killed by them.

caught, and instantly torn to pieces before Fanny's face, who was unable to assist it with any aid more powerful than pity; nor could she prevail on Joseph, who had been himself a sportsman in his youth, to attempt any thing contrary to the laws of hunting, in favour of the hare, which he said was killed fairly.

The hare was caught within a yard or two of Adams, who lay asleep at some distance from the lovers; and the hounds in devouring it, and pulling it backwards and forwards, had drawn it so close to him, that some of them (by mistake perhaps for the hare's skin) laid hold of the skirts of his cassock; others at the same time applying their teeth to his wig, which he had with a handkerchief fastened to his head, began to pull him about; and had not the motion of his body had more effect on him than seemed to be wrought by the noise, they must certainly have tasted his flesh, which delicious flavour might have been fatal to him: but being roused by these tuggings, he instantly awaked, and with a jerk delivering his head from his wig, he with most admirable dexterity recovered his legs, which now seemed the only members he could entrust his safety to . . .

No sooner did Joseph Andrews perceive the distress of his friend, when first the quick-scenting dogs attacked him, than he grasped his cudgel in his right-hand, a cudgel which his father had of his grand-father, to whom a mighty strong man of Kent had given it for a present in that day when he broke three heads on the stage. It was a cudgel of mighty strength and wonderful art, made by one of Mr. Deard's best workmen whom no other artificer can equal, and who hath made all those sticks which the beaus have lately walked with about the Park in a morning: but this was far his master-piece; on its head was engraved a nose and chin, which might have been mistaken for a pair of nutcrack-ers. The learned have imagined it designed to represent the Gorgon: but it was in fact copied from the face of a certain long English baronet of infinite wit, humour, and gravity . . .

No sooner had Joseph grasped this cudgel in his hands, than lightning darted from his eyes; and the heroick youth, swift of foot, ran with the utmost speed to his friend's assistance. He overtook him just as Rock-wood had laid hold of the skirt of his cassock, which being torn hung to the ground. Reader, we would make a simile on this occasion, but for two reasons: The first is, it would interrupt the description which should be rapid in this part; but that doth not weigh much, many pre-cedents occurring for such an interruption: The second and much greater reason is, that we could find no simile adequate to our purpose: for indeed what instance could we bring to set before our reader's eyes

at once the idea of friendship, courage, youth, beauty, strength, and swiftness; all which blazed in the person of Joseph Andrews. Let those therefore that describe lions and tigers, and heroes fiercer than both, raise their poems or plays with the simile of Joseph Andrews, who is himself above the reach of any simile.

Now Rockwood had laid fast hold on the parson's skirts, and stopt his flight; which Joseph no sooner perceived, than he levelled his cudgel at his head, and laid him sprawling. Jowler and Ringwood then fell on his greatcoat, and had undoubtedly brought him to the ground, had not Joseph, collecting all his force, given Jowler such a rap on the back, that quitting his hold he ran howling over the plain. A harder fate remained for thee, O Ringwood, Ringwood the best hound that ever pursued a hare, who never threw his tongue but where the scent was undoubtedly true; good at trailing, and sure in a highway; no babbler, no over-runner, respected by the whole pack, who, whenever he opened, knew the game was at hand. He fell by the stroke of Joseph. Thunder, and Plunder, and Wonder, and Blunder, were the next victims of his wrath, and measured their length on the ground. Then Fairmaid, a bitch

13. YELLOWHAM WOOD, COUNTY OF DORSET

From a print dedicated to J. J. Farquharson, Esq, engraved by H. Alken and R. G. Reeve from original drawings by W. P. Hodges, Esq, and published on November 1st, 1834 by Thos. McLean, London. 19½ins × 12½ins

Yellowham Wood, in Dorset, is the same Yell'am Wood that appears, with Yell'am Firs, in some of the poems and stories of Thomas Hardy. It lies about five miles east of Dorchester, and a mile south of the village of Puddletown, in the Cattistock Hunt country. The Hunt, which used to be called the Blue Hunt, was started towards the end of the eighteenth century by the Rev. W. Phelips, and J. J. Farquharson, to whom this print is dedicated, was Master for over fifty years, from 1806-1858. The Cattistock was one of the earlier Hunts, formed half a century before fox-hunting became the most important and popular form of hunting in the British Isles. As a lighter and faster riding horse was developed, capable of sustaining a good speed and of jumping considerable obstacles, it was natural that the country gentleman should prefer a faster type of hunting, and the fox could be driven fast and straight over open country. Its pursuers were given the opportunity to display their courage and skill in a way that was not possible in the woods with staghounds or coursing in the fields. Today there are about two hundred packs of foxhounds, and about sixty which hunt hares.

The artist was born Walter Parry, and took the name Hodges as the condition of a bequest in an uncle's will. He was a gentleman painter, whose best-known work was the set *The Beaufort Hunt*, and his engraving was done by Henry Alken, a great draughtsman.

From Original Drawings by W. P. HODGES. ESQ.ᴿ

YELLOWHAM WOOD.

Engraved by H. ALKEN and R. G. REEVE.

which Mr. John Temple had bred up in his house, and fed at his own table, and lately sent the squire fifty miles for a present, ran fiercely at Joseph, and bit him by the leg; no dog was ever fiercer than she, being descended from an Amazonian breed, and had worried bulls in her own country, but now waged an unequal fight; and had shared the fate of those we have mentioned before, had not Diana (the reader may believe or not as he pleases) in that instant interposed, and in the shape of the huntsman snatched her favourite up in her arms.

The parson now faced about, and with his crabstick felled many to the earth, and scattered others, till he was attacked by Caesar, and pulled to the ground. Then Joseph flew to his rescue, and with such might fell on the victor, that, O eternal blot to his name! Caesar ran yelping away.

The battle now raged with the most dreadful violence, when lo! the huntsman, a man of years and dignity, lifted his voice, and called his hounds from the fight; telling them, in a language they understood, that it was in vain to contend longer; for that fate had decreed the victory to their enemies.

LARKING

From *Life of John Mytton* by Nimrod, 1837

But it has not been in this run, nor in that run, in one country or in another country, that Mytton has made himself signal; and yet I might hazard an imputation on my veracity were I to recount *all* the extraordinary deeds of this most extraordinary man, in various situations with hounds. Indeed, adding the hazards for his neck that he has encountered in the field to those to which he has subjected himself elsewhere, the most extraordinary thing after all is, that he is at this moment in existence. However, confining my remarks to his riding, I am bound to pronounce him one of the most *daring* horsemen that ever came under my eye; and I must likewise add that, all things considered, he has had fewer falls, and tired fewer horses in chase, than his larking and desperate system of crossing countries would warrant the expectation of. But this has been attributable to the immense muscular powers of the man; to a sort of iron grasp by which he holds his horses in his hand at all times, and upon all occasions, which, let your slack-rein gentlemen say what they may, is no small support to a horse going *his* (Mytton's) pace over a country, and particularly over the uneven sur-

face, the deep ditches, and blind grips of his own county, Shropshire. Indeed, when I last met him, I asked him whether it had ever been his fate so to tire a hunter as not to be able to ride him home, when he declared he never recollected having done so. As to the height and width of fences which have been ridden over by him, I repeat I am afraid to recapitulate them; but I have very respectable attestation to my having once measured a brook that he rode Baronet over, in cold blood, in my presence, on our way home from hunting, and found it exceed, by some inches, nine yards from hind-foot to hind-foot! He afterwards backed Baronet to clear nine yards over hurdles placed at some distance from each other; but he performed the task so often with him before the appointed time, that the horse refused it, and lost his master's money. In Lord Bradford's Park he cleared one of his Lordship's deer-hurdles, upwards of six feet high! and, what is more surprising, he covered the space of eight yards in length at the same time. This was accomplished on a horse called Hero, which he purchased of me for 500 guineas, and was the same that leaped the gate with him in Mr. Jellico's grounds in Shropshire, the height of which was seven feet. But far from pleasing reflections are the result of looking back upon these brilliant feats of horsemanship, rarely excelled by any one. On the contrary, we cannot help lamenting that a person so gifted to shine in the field, as Mr. Mytton proved himself to be, should not have taken more care to preserve, unimpaired, the almost unequalled natural powers which he possessed, – so essential to the figure he made.

123. *Above* 'Our friend Mr Noddy has a day with the Brookside Harriers – with his usual prudence he gets his horse accustomed to the hills,' from *Hunting – Incidents of the Noble Science* by John Leech, published in 1865.

124. *Left* From *Hunting – Incidents of the Noble Science* by John Leech, published in 1865. Leech worked for Punch from its foundation in 1841 until his death, and these drawings originally appeared as woodcuts in that magazine.

WILD MELTONIANS
AND OTHER HAZARDS

From Squire Osbaldeston: His Autobiography, 1787-1866

One of the greatest difficulties to be contended with in the Quorn country (other than the Meltonian practice of riding over the hounds and heading foxes!) was the behaviour of the stocking-makers and weavers, who used to assemble in crowds at the covert-side. It seemed impossible to keep them together in the right place in order to let the fox go away. At first we could not manage them at all; we tried persuasion and kind words, without any success. Then we tried force; but being totally unsupported by any of the Meltonians that method also failed. At last we had recourse to bribery; we used to give every village two sovereigns a year for drink, and this plan had a far better effect, though on occasions the people were still unruly.

Another exceedingly vexatious habit these people had was their Sunday pastime of collecting terriers and curs to hunt our coverts. I frequently sent my two whippers-in, accompanied by local persons who knew the intruders, to warn them that hunting with dogs on Sunday was an offence punishable by fine, and they might even get into prison. This served to deter a good many, and after a time only a few of the more hardened spirits attempted it. Some bad feeling remained, however, and in the end resulted in a fight between myself, one of my whippers-in and a little man who lived in the neighbourhood on the one side, and the stocking-makers on the other; and the fight ended in a general row. We came off victorious, but it was a wonder we were not nearly killed.

The affair occurred in a village called Sileby, which was full of stocking-makers, and only three miles from Quorn. We met annually on the first Monday in November at Kirby Gate, which is two miles or a little more from Melton Mowbray, the celebrated resort of the wild Meltonians, and on the turnpike road to Leicester. We used always to draw Cream Lodge Gorse, near Ashby Pastures, a famous covert; we only cub-hunted the coverts in the open country once, and then only those which we knew held a litter of foxes.

It was the case here; a large field were out, and very wild and unruly; also the foxes were young: these united circumstances destroyed all chance of a run and we had very little sport. I almost always took the hounds home myself, and I did so in this instance. Of course, I was very much annoyed at the day's doings and not in a very amiable temper.

As we frequently ran the foxes to ground in drains, almost every field in Leicestershire being hollow-drained, we always took a terrier with us and left him shut up in some place as conveniently situated for the coverts we intended to draw as we could judge. This precaution was necessary because some of the mad-headed Meltonians would certainly have ridden over the little unfortunate animal if he had run with the hounds. On this occasion I had sent my second whipper-in for the terrier, the place where we had left him being some distance out of our road to Quorn; in consequence, my only companions were my whipper-in, Stevens, and the little man I have mentioned – I forget his name. Sileby was in our road home; and soon after we entered the village two men with a sort of bulldog came out of a public house and began kicking and striking the hounds. They lamed one or two of them. I immediately said: 'What right have you to kick the hounds. I'll give you something you won't like if you repeat that game!' One of them answered with abuse, saying he would knock me off my horse. I had a hunting whip made of cane, the butt not at all heavy, only sufficient to open a gate, which was fortunate, as the sequel will show. The man came round to me, took hold of my bridle and seized my leg, meaning to pull me off. I allowed him to do so because I thus had a better purchase to stand up and hit him over the head. Notwithstanding my whip was rather light, I hit him so hard two or three times that I cut his hat open and his head bled a good deal. Finding that he had the worst of it and could not get me off he bolted.

Whilst the fellow was attacking me his companion attacked Stevens, wrenched his whip away, and holding it with both hands struck Stevens's head. He missed his mark but knocked one of the horses' eyes clean out, so that nothing remained but the empty socket. Had my whip been furnished with a handle as heavy as Stevens' I might have killed my antagonist; Stevens' would knock off any padlock. As soon as the poor horse lost his eye he began neighing and plunged to such an extent that his assailant bolted after his friend. We immediately gave chase, and saw the two run into another public house. By this time 40 or 50 stocking-makers had collected and began abusing us. Stevens jumped off his horse, and giving it to the little man to hold, rushed into the public house after the two, meaning to find out who they were.

My horse was rather shy and seemed afraid of the people, but after a touch of the spurs he would have gone at anything. One or two of the blackguards talked of attacking me, and one came too close. I rode at him and knocked him end over end. While these encounters were going on the hounds were sitting looking at us; but no further attempt was

125. A hunting breakfast, by Thomas Rowlandson, c. 1790.

made to ill-use them. I have often thought since that we were very lucky to come off as well as we did; had the whole mob joined in the attack upon us we might have been killed.

As soon as Stevens, having failed in his errand, came out of the public house, I addressed the crowd in nearly the following words: 'I rather think you have mistaken me for one of my whippers-in. I am the Master of the Hounds, and you must know that I live at Quorn. If any two of you will come to Quorn tomorrow morning about eleven o'clock, and will identify the two ruffians who assaulted us, and will swear to them, I will give you five pounds.' (The mistake might easily arise as I wore a cap.)

I did not expect any of them would come, but two men made their appearance next morning and told me who the fellows were. I consulted a gentleman by the name of Craddock, a solicitor who hunted constantly with us, and also collected the subscriptions and paid the rents of the coverts and expenses of earth-stopping; but we did not agree as to the best mode of proceeding against our assailants. I was for endeavouring to obtain redress for the damage done to the horse; he was for prosecuting them for a violent assault; and considering his judgment better than mine I gave way. The men were arrested and tried at Quarter Sessions; the two informants kept their word to me and swore to the prisoners' identity; and on conviction each was sentenced to six months' imprisonment and hard labour. This had a good effect which lasted for a considerable time. One of the men convicted was a carpenter and a desperate character who was afterwards transported for attempting the life of a constable in the execution of his duty.

Near the close of my career in Leicestershire we had another row of a different kind. It happened in the Harborough country, and our opponents were very much of the same character as the Sileby stocking-makers. We had had only a short burst of about a quarter of an hour when the fox went to ground in Hallaton Bottoms; as we did not know where to find another fox, and the one which had gone to ground could not have been tired, we determined to get him out, particularly as the drain was only a short one. About 20 stocking-makers and similar people collected and assisted the second whipper-in to get the fox out; and after twenty minutes' work they bagged him, having a sack in their possession. We turned him down and gave him two fields start, but I think he must have been hurt in the process of getting out of the drain, for he could not run and hounds ran into him in less than a mile.

The terrier we put into the drain had remained there, and my whipper-in, hearing him at bay, thought there must be another fox; so,

having killed the one we went back. Before we reached the spot, however, we learned that it was a badger the terrier had bayed; and when we arrived the men had got him out and put him into their sack. We had some young terriers at home and wanted the badger to try them with; and as the fellows had been liberally paid for their help in getting out the fox I felt that we were entitled to claim the badger; so I asked the men to give it to my whipper-in. They refused and cursed us freely. Sebright, my first whipper-in, got off his horse and tried civil persuasion, whereupon one of the men knocked him down. That made an end

126. *Village scenery – hounds going to cover* by Dean Wolstenholme (1757–1837), engraved by Dean Wolstenholme Jnr. One of a series of prints of the Hertfordshire Hunt: a view near Offley.

kept my eye upon him and soon caught him up in the covert. He dropped the sack and seized hold of my bridle. I rose in my stirrups and hit him on the hands with the butt end of my whip, which made him quickly let go. Then I gave him a few hard knocks with my fist and drove him off. The whippers-in came at my call and took the badger, while the men from a respectable distance swore at us, saying they would kill all the foxes and uttered other threats. The covert belonged to the Rev. Mr. Bewick, who frequently hunted with us; he was a good friend to fox-hunting, and was also a magistrate; so I told the men I should report their threats to him.

No attempt was made to destroy the foxes; we always found when we drew that covert as we had done before the row.

Two other incidents may be worth recording. Near Ashby Pastures an old crusty, cross-grained farmer occupied a few fields close to the covert. He was always grumbling, though we scarcely ever crossed one of them once in a year. He never discharged us and we never contemplated that he would resort to such disgraceful means of revenge. Cream Lodge Gorse was not above a mile from his land; a most celebrated covert and a certain find. He put poison in and about it, but of

127. *A Stone in the Hoof* by Thomas Rowlandson, 1781.

of endeavours to negotiate, and determined me to have the badger. As soon as Sebright had picked himself up I called him and the second whipper-in and told them to remount. When they had done so I bade them keep their reins tight so that they could not be caught hold of, and we would charge the men in line.

The gang were moving off by this time and were about 50 yards away. We put our horses into a gallop and were upon them before they guessed our intention. Taken by surprise they scattered and ran in different directions, but we knocked several of them down before they could get away. The man who carried the badger ran as well as he could for his load, towards a thick grass covert, thinking we could not follow. I had

14. GROUSE SHOOTING

From a drawing by Samuel Howett. 17ins × 12ins

This shooting piece is set away from the woodland to which Howett was so attached, on the grouse moors of Scotland or the north of England. He liked to draw animals, and understood the character of these dogs as well as that of the spaniels in his *Pheasant Shooting* (plate 3). These pointers are stronger, rangier and built for a hard day's work over long distances – for shooting grouse was no easy enjoyment. A sporting clergyman, the Reverend W. B. Daniel, wrote of it: 'Upon the hills, where a *horse* can travel, this is a noble diversion; to be undertaken otherwise demands constant and hard labour, for the Shooter is, during the course of the day, *ascending,* that is, if he finds a *brood* on the top of one eminence, they will sweep over the valley, until they reach the summit of another, up which the Sportsman has to climb.' The Shooters were not deterred by these difficulties, however, and the killing of grouse became on occasion more of a wholesale slaughter than a sport. Gilbert White of Selborne protested against the 'unreasonable sportsmen who killed in 1740 to 1741 as many as twenty brace of partridges in Wolmer Forest.' What would he have thought of the record bag for one gun, which stands to the credit – if credit is the word – of Lord Walsingham, who in one September day in 1888, at Blubberhouse in Yorkshire, killed 1,070 birds.

In Howett's day the arrangements for shoots were very crude. For days before, a veritable army of men with nets and dogs would surround an area of country, and, gradually closing in, drive everything before it. They would then trap the game within high nets, and the shooters, provided with six guns or more apiece, would kill every living creature which escaped.

Grouse Shooting

course we were perfectly ignorant of it. He knew the day we should draw it, so that the poison could not have lost any of its power. We found as usual and went away, but whether we had a good run or not I don't remember. However, in a few hours after reaching Quorn, my kennel huntsman came to me in the evening and said, 'Sir, three couples of hounds which were out to-day are very ill indeed and I am afraid will die.'

Of course I was very much annoyed; we applied every remedy we could think of, but two died in a few hours after his announcement, being very much convulsed. Their appearance created suspicion and I sent for the doctor; he opened them and said they had been poisoned. By his treatment, however, we saved the others. Two more which were among the pack had not returned home, and we were certain that they had shared the same fate. I sent one of my men to see if he could discover the lost ones in or about Cream Lodge Gorse, and he did. One was dead close to it and the other a few fields off, so I suppose the poor creature had struggled as long as it could to follow the pack.

There was a very gallant colonel who had distinguished himself in many actions as a cavalry officer and constantly hunted with my hounds. Notwithstanding the diabolical conduct of the old farmer, we had the courage to draw the covert some time afterwards again. It so happened that the colonel and I were obliged to cross one of his fields with several others. There was a flight of rails into it, and the hounds running very hard at the time, there was no time for reflection. To our great dismay and surprise we saw at some distance before we reached them old 'Cerberus' with a pitchfork in his hand and another man with a similar weapon standing on the opposite side of the rails, ready to receive us. The colonel said, 'Charge them in line!' which, although it appeared a most dangerous experiment, we did; and most miraculously, after knocking our two antagonists over we galloped on without receiving any injury. I have often thought since what an extraordinary escape we had.

Through the intervention of several influential farmers adjoining old 'Cerberus's' land all hatred, malice and uncharitableness ceased, and we hunted in future without any molestation.

THE INSENSIBLE SPORTSMAN

Letter to The Spectator reprinted in the *Gentlemen's Magazine* 1736

Mr Spectator,

About this Time Twelvemonth I was, against my Inclination, marry'd to one of the greatest Sportsmen, in as great a sporting Country as any in *England*: I was immediately ravish'd from dear, dear *London*, to an old Mansion-House, situated between two Woods; was forced from the *Opera*, and the *Masquerade*, to live among the *Yelpings* of *Hounds*, the *Noise* of *Horns*, and eternal debates about *Horses*. How disagreeable this was to me you may easily imagine, and how affecting the Joys of Matrimony were when the Husband and Wife had such different notions of living. He lov'd the *Country*, I languish'd for the *Town*; I hated *Solitude*, and he *Assemblies*: He cou'd not endure *Quadrille*, nor I *Backgammon*; I lik'd to lie a Bed 'till *Ten*, and he was always up by *Three* or *Four*. Notwithstanding these natural Antipathies as I was his Wife I tacitly conform'd, and did all in my Power to be an agreeable Companion: he seem'd mighty fond for a Week, but the Season being begun, he had other Business than to regard a *Wife*. He soon deserted me, to follow a *Hare*, and left the safe Embraces of my Arms, to venture his Neck in the Pursuit of a *Fox*; this Neglect of me encreas'd as the Season more and more advanced, and I had soon the Torture to see myself rivall'd by his *Hounds* and his *Horses*: Ringwood was oftener kiss'd than his *Spouse*, and *Whitefoot* had more of his *Conversation*. Even a *rainy Day* made no Alteration; for when he could not be in the *Field*, he was either in the *Kennel* or *Stable*, consulting with the *Groom*, or giving Orders to the *Huntsman*: And if he was within the House he was *drinking* with Sportsmen, or *damning* the *Weather*, or in a sullen ill-nature finding Fault with the whole Family – Such was my Happiness all last Winter, such I expect this, and such, in some Respect or other, is the hard Usage of all the Sportsmen's Wives in *Great Britain* – Now, Mr. *Spec*, I think it Incumbent on you, to write a *Paper* in some Manner to reclaim these *wild Savages*, and give them a Hint that a *Woman* is far more preferable than a *Fox*.

In the meantime please to insert the following Dialogue, occasion'd by a young Gentleman of this Country leaving his Bride at 4 next Morning after he was married, to hunt with Ld *Volpone*.

Suffolk   *Your humble Servant,*
Sept. 1.   LYDIA RANGER

128. The noble science, from *Hunting – Incidents of the Noble Science* by John Leech, published in 1865.

129. *Above* The racehorse Anticipation – foaled in 1812, the chestnut son of Hambletonian. He was one of the strongest and best horses of his day, winning the Ascot Gold Cup in 1816 and 1819.

130. *Right An extraordinary match by George Osbaldeston Esq.* by Henry Alken, engraved by George Hunt and published in 1831. On the Saturday of the Houghton meeting at Newmarket in 1831, Squire Osbaldeston backed himself with 1000 guineas to ride 200 miles in 10 hours. He started his journey at 7.13 in the morning, changing horses after each 4 miles. After the 14th and 25th rounds he took a little brandy and water, and after 120 miles he dismounted and ate a little cold partridge. At 9 minutes to 4 he won his bet, amid riotously enthusiastic scenes, by completing the 200 miles in 8 hours 39 minutes.

RACING

MULE-RACING

From *Life on the Mississippi* by Mark Twain, 1883

There were thirteen mules in the first heat; all sorts of mules, they were; all sorts of complexions, gaits, dispositions, aspects. Some were handsome creatures, some were not; some were sleek, some hadn't had their fur brushed lately; some were innocently gay and frisky; some were full of malice and all unrighteousness; guessing from looks, some of them thought the matter on hand was war, some thought it was a lark, the rest took it for a religious occasion. And each mule acted according to his convictions. The result was an absence of harmony well compensated by a conspicuous presence of variety – variety of a picturesque and entertaining sort.

All the riders were young gentlemen in fashionable society. If the reader has been wondering why it is that the ladies of New Orleans attend so humble an orgy as a mule-race, the thing is explained now. It is a fashion-freak; all connected with it are people of fashion.

It is great fun, and cordially liked. The mule-race is one of the marked occasions of the year. It has brought some pretty fast mules to the front. One of these had to be ruled out, because he was so fast that he turned the thing into a one-mule contest, and robbed it of one of its best features – variety. But every now and then somebody disguises him with a new name and a new complexion, and brings him in again.

The riders dress in full jockey costumes of bright-coloured silks, satins, and velvets.

The thirteen mules got away in a body, after a couple of false starts, and scampered off with prodigious spirit. As each mule and each rider had a distinct opinion of his own as to how the race ought to be run, and which side of the track was best in certain circumstances, and how often the track ought to be crossed, and when a collision ought to be accomplished, and when it ought to be avoided, these twenty-six conflicting opinions created a most fantastic and picturesque confusion, and the resulting spectacle was killingly comical.

Mile heat; time 2.22. Eight of the thirteen mules distanced. I had a

bet on a mule which would have won if the procession had been reversed. The second heat was good fun; and so was the 'consolation race for beaten mules,' which followed later; but the first heat was the best in that respect.

I think that much the most enjoyable of all races is a steamboat race; but, next to that, I prefer the gay and joyous mule-rush. Two red-hot steamboats raging along, neck-and-neck, straining every nerve – that is to say, every rivet in the boilers – quaking and shaking and groaning from stem to stern, spouting white steam from the pipes, pouring black smoke from the chimneys, raining down sparks, parting the river into long breaks of hissing foam – this is sport that makes a body's very liver curl with enjoyment. A horse-race is pretty tame and colourless in comparison. Still, a horse-race might be well enough, in its way, perhaps if it were not for the tiresome false starts. But then, nobody is ever killed. At least, nobody was ever killed when I was at a horse-race. They have been crippled, it is true; but this is little to the purpose.

CLINKER *v* CLASHER

From *Squire Osbaldeston: His Autobiography*, 1787-1866

The sixth and last steeple-chase match I rode was made under the following circumstances: Captain Becher was very sore at his defeat on General Charritie's grey, and after that match was continually singing the praises of Clinker. I had a bay horse I called Clasher, which I bought

off a farmer in Lord Yarborough's country; whether he was a thoroughbred I don't know, but he had all the appearance of it. He was an extraordinary fencer, a capital water-jumper, and very fast. One day after dinner Becher was vaunting the merits of Clinker, and I said I would run him with Clasher. He laughed, evidently thinking I meant it as a joke; but finding I was in earnest he came to terms and the match was made, I stipulating that if Clasher should be lame it was void. It so happened that I did lame him while hunting my hounds, and the match was accordingly postponed. Clinker in the meantime had passed into the hands of Captain Ross, who sent him to be sold at Tattersall's on a Monday. I happened to look in on the Sunday and met several men I knew who chaffed me, saying I had been afraid to run against Clinker after all. I explained why the match had not come off, and no more was said.

Next day, two or three hours before Tattersall's sale began, Colonel Anson, Ross, myself and two or three others met to shoot pigeons at the Red House, Battersea. As soon as Ross saw me he began chaffing: 'You have been crabbing my horse to injure the sale of him,' he said, 'and you know you didn't dare run him, though you told people you weren't afraid to!' When I laughed, telling him it was not too late to make the match now, Ross took me up at once in good earnest, saying if I really meant it he would send a messenger to Tattersall's to countermand the sale. The upshot was that he withdrew the horse from the list, and we signed Articles for a thousand a side, five miles across country, even weights; the event to come off immediately after the York Spring Assizes (I was High Sheriff for Yorkshire that year 1829 and was consequently obliged to attend the Assizes). Ross stipulated that I should ride my own horse; I was hunting Northamptonshire at that time, and was rather vexed with myself for having agreed to this, because, hunting hounds myself, there was always the chance of a fall which might disable me and forbid my riding the match, in which case I should have to forfeit the whole £1,000, the terms being p.p.; and I stood all the money myself.

It was inserted in the Articles that we were both to go over the line before starting. This we did the day before the match with the late Sir Harry Goodriche, who was my umpire, and Captain White, who was Ross's. There were two brooks, one of which was wide, the other a mere nothing. Somebody remarking that the former was a pretty big jump, Goodriche made light of it, saying he could do it on the horse he was riding. He rode at the brook three or four times, but his horse would not look at it.

As I knew the line thoroughly I agreed with my head groom that I

should make the running. We started near Dalby on the Melton side and finished within a quarter of a mile of Tilton-on-the-Hill, one of the finest lines in Leicestershire, and very severe, being hilly, high-ridged furrow, and deep. I forgot to mention that Dick Christian, one of the best riders of that day, rode Clinker. About half-way was Sir Harry's brook, and in the same field was a haystack, and the best place to take the brook was to leave the stack on the left hand. While going up a strong hill on the same field, before reaching the haystack, Christian said, 'I beat you, for a hundred!' Turning my head, I saw him bearing to the other end of the field and shouted, 'Where are you riding to? This is the line!' At the same time I saw a man on horseback close to the brook. I afterwards discovered that there was a ford which they had found the day before, but I knew nothing about it. Christian walked Clinker

131. *In and Out* by Henry Alken Jnr., engraved by Charles Hunt and published in *Sheldon's National Sports*.

opposite to it; and the moment the fellow saw I was in front he hid himself in the ditch. I saw him under my feet, for luckily I determined to go at the first opening I saw, and it happened to be the right one. At this moment Christian's horse's nose nearly touched the tail of mine. We had to turn short to the left and jump a moderate fence into the winning field, and went at it almost abreast. His horse was so dreadfully distressed that he tumbled into it, and I cantered on to the winning chair. My horse was much distressed also; so much that I thought at the time, '*If I can clear this last fence I shall win*,' because the ground Christian had lost, going wide to that ford and crossing the molehill field, besides the pace I had ridden, must have beaten him.

Clinker could not get up for 20 minutes; he lay groaning, and staling all around him.

15. DONCASTER RACES: RACE FOR THE GREAT ST. LEGER STAKES, 1836. VEXATION – THE FALSE START

From a print after James Pollard, engraved by J. Harris and published on May 24th, 1837 by Ackermann & Co., London. 25ins × 18⅛ins

The St. Leger is one of the five classic races of the English turf, the others being the One Thousand Guineas, the Two Thousand Guineas, the Oaks and the Derby. It was established in 1776, and named after Lieut.-General Anthony St. Leger, who first had the idea for the race. It is run at the beginning of September at Doncaster, over a distance of one mile, six furlongs and 132 yards, and is open to both colts and fillies. The Leger is reckoned to be the peak of the career of a classic three-year-old, and on the morning and evening of each day of the St. Leger week there is a sale of yearlings that nowadays brings bloodstock breeders from all over the world. The Yorkshiremen of Doncaster consider the race to be the most important of the year. They say: 'The fittest horse wins the Guineas, the luckiest horse wins the Derby, but the best horse wins the Leger.' It is the only classic to be run in the north of England – the other four are at Newmarket or Epsom.

The St. Leger of 1836 was won by Lord George Bentinck's colt Elis. Lord George was a great owner and a great gambler – and also, it seems, a man of some ingenuity. In the early years of the nineteenth century, the transport of horses to distant meetings was a considerable problem, and they were often hacked over long distances. It was Lord George who had the revolutionary idea of a horse box on wheels – the one in the background at the left of the picture. He took the colt Elis to Doncaster in it, and caused great agitation among the bookmakers. Their spies had informed them that Elis was still in his stable at Goodwood a few days before the race, and could not possibly reach the course in time. They laid against Elis accordingly, and Lord George made a great deal of money. This was one of his many successes against the bookies, but in spite of determined efforts he never succeeded in breaking the ring. Nor did he ever achieve his great ambition of winning the Derby. In 1846, after a lifetime in racing, he suddenly decided to sell all his horses and devote himself to politics. One of the horses he sold, Surplice, won the Derby two years after he parted with it.

132. *Above* Colonel Thornton, a classic example of the all-round sportsman of the Regency period. Born in 1773, his interests ranged from falconry to athletics, but his first love was shooting. He owned three 150-guinea guns, which he named Death, Destruction and Fate.

133. *Top right* The Derby, Epsom, 26th May, 1875. The crowd in the foreground show little interest in the race, where Galopin, the 2-1 favourite, can be seen coming up to the finish ahead of Claremont. Galopin was owned by Prince Batthyany, an immensely popular racing figure, who died in 1884 in the Jockey Club luncheon-room, fatally over-excited at the prospect of the 2000 guineas being won by Galopin's son, Galliard.

through it, and lost the race by doing so. My horse cleared the water with about a yard to spare. The next field was a large one and hilly, and covered with molehills. There was a sheep track in the direct line, and I made all sail along it. Christian lost about 60 yards by walking through the brook, and having to gallop uphill over the molehills.

He nearly caught me at the end of the field, but I knew he must have distressed his horse, and made as strong running as I could down to the next brook. We had then to rise another hilly field which was within two of the winning post. There was a baulk, as they call it, along a hedgeside, and through this hedge was an opening which was the only practicable way out of the field. It was so intricate that we had agreed to place a man

LONDON, PUBLISHED MAY 24TH 1837, BY ACKERMANN & CO 96, STRAND.

RACE FOR THE GREAT St. LEGER STAKES, 1836.

Vexation——The false Start.

THE TOUTER

From *Turf Characters* by Martingale, 1851

The Touter arrives at the scene of action some days previous to the commencement of the races, for the especial purpose of watching all the movements which may take place. These are duly reported to the parties by whom he is employed and remunerated, and who reside probably at a considerable distance from the scene of action. In all his proceedings he is extremely alert, and can catch at the least indication of any forthcoming change. He attends the public training ground regularly, and knows every horse; but appears, to a mere observer, to take little notice of what is going forward. His visits to the private training-ground, however, are paid by stealth,–by secreting himself in the bottom of the hedge or the ditches of the ground, or, perhaps, an adjoining plantation, especially if he has, by some means or other, possessed himself of the information that some great trial is about to take place before the break of day. His retreat, under these circumstances, is difficult to be discovered, as he has, perhaps, been out all night; but, when that is the case, he is liable to meet with a severe horsewhipping, if any one has courage enough to encounter him. To each horse, particularly the favourites in betting, he pays the most marked attention. Nor is he, from his long experience, a bad judge of the capabilities of a racer. He can mark in a moment if there be 'a screw loose' in any of the respective competitors. He notes also whether they have done their work regularly, –whether, on pulling up, there is the slightest indication of a cough,– whether such an one does not go with his accustomed ease and temper,– or whether there is the least appearance of lameness. Nor is he less attentive to the sweats,–the manner, particularly, in which each horse goes through that important and necessary operation. But in case of a breakdown (as, for instance, Sultan did before the St. Leger), he is all bustle and activity. All the information which he thus picks up by incessant attention and untiring watchfulness, is communicated to his employers, and they act accordingly. When Sultan broke down on Doncaster race-ground, a day or two previous to the decision of the great event of the week, the Touter was the first to mark it; and although Mr. Crockford immediately set off for London in a chaise and four, the information despatched by the Touter would not be far behind that important personage. This may be taken as an instance upon which he particularly prides himself.

On the other hand, the Touter, who is easily distinguished by his costume,–half groom, half wayfarer,–is always upon good terms with himself, and, as occasion serves, can indulge in a little brag. He can boast of an acquaintance with many important personages,–how he has tasted turtle-soup and drank champagne, especially if he has been successful in pointing out a winner,–a fortunate circumstance which not only brings to him an additional supply of the needful, but wonderfully raises his own reputation as a good judge. This self-importance leads him to mention names in a manner which implies that he is on terms of the closest familiarity with the greatest betters and the first jockeys of the day, as if, indeed, they were his most intimate associates, than which nothing can be further from the truth.

Nevertheless, there is much virtue in experience; and if the Touter knows the precise state of the odds, by hanging about the precincts of the

134. *The Starting Field:* one of a set of six prints by Henry Alken, engraved by J. Harris and published in *Fores's Steeplechase Scenes* in 1848.

besides, he is as fat as a bullock. Now with his bad fore legs, his weight of flesh, and 8 st. 7 lbs. upon his back, depend upon it he will never reach home.' It turned out as the Touter had predicted, with this exception, that Cobham broke down near the distance and not at the end of the white rails, as he had said. The same Touter was equally correct in the following year with regard to Bloomsbury, and afterwards as to Charles XII.

The life of the Touter, however, like many of those who move in a higher sphere, has its vicissitudes. But he carries about with him a wonderful elasticity of spirit, and fully exemplifies in his own person what the force of habit can accomplish; for although the colour of his garments is changeable, year by year, as the hues of autumn, he cannot divest himself of the propensity of annually visiting scenes which his second nature has rendered attractive and interesting, however much he may be borne down by the occurrence of any unfortunate or adventitious circumstance. His heart is affianced to the very turf itself. The splendour of morning, the freshness of the breeze as it sweeps over the race-ground, the cry of the snipe or the call of the plover, may be disregarded or fall dead upon his ear. But he loves the turf for its old and many associations, abounding with the reminiscences of victory after victory, defeat after defeat; and, glancing through the future, he can see, or fancies that he sees, a succession of events more important than those which he has witnessed, and more worthy of being placed on the page of the turf's annals. Thus the long-continued habits of the Touter can be no more shaken off, than can those which pertain to a higher calling and a more liberal remuneration. And if he pries into the secrets of others, watchful early and late, letting not the most trivial circumstance escape his observation, but, at the same time, placing no reliance upon mere hearsay, and guided solely by the facts which come under his own eye, he is only pursuing a vocation which may be as fully justified as many which bear a far more imposing name than that of the Touter.

STEEPLE-CHASE FOR ONE THOUSAND SOVEREIGNS

From *Pierce Egan's Book of Sports*, 1832

The match between Moonraker, the property of Mr. Elmore, and Grimaldi, the property of Mr. Evans, came off on Tuesday, 13th March, 1832, according to appointment, in the neighbourhood of Harrow. This

135. *Racing at Newmarket* by F. Sartorius, 1767. Bay Malton beating King Herod, Turf and Askam for a sweepstake of 500 guineas over the Beacon Course at Newmarket on April 21st, 1767. This painting, by the best known member of the Sartorius family, measures 6 ft. 3 ins. × 4 ft. 1 in.

betting-room, and assumes a knowledge of matters which he does not possess, on many occasions he is remarkably accurate as to the result of the forthcoming great event. A remarkable instance of accuracy of observation and opinion took place with one of this 'honourable' fraternity in the year 1838. A person, to whom he was in some measure known, said to the race-course loiterer, on the Saturday night previous to the Doncaster race week, 'Well, what's to win?'–'Don John,' answered the Touter. 'Ion will be second, and Cobham will break down at the end of the white rails opposite the Intake farm.'–'What? Can you say positively that Don John will win?'–'Yes, I can; for there's never a horse in all Doncaster can go with him–depend upon it.'–'How can you tell that?'–'Never mind how I can tell. I tell you it will be so: Ion will be second, and it will be with Cobham just as I have said.'–'But what are your reasons that Cobham will break down–it seems strange that you can tell that.'–'The reasons,' rejoined the Touter, 'are these. Cobham is bad in his fore legs. He has not had a rattling gallop for many a day;

match was made on the evening of Thursday week, at St. Albans, after the grand Sweepstakes which were run for on that day, when Moonraker and Grimaldi contested the ground with such vigour. Each party was equally confident that in a fresh trial his horse would be successful, and such was Mr. Osbaldeston's high opinion of Grimaldi, that he actually gave, or rather promised to give, Mr. Elmore 50*l*. to make the match, thus placing Grimaldi in the stakes a favourite at 550*l*. to 450*l*. Notwithstanding this position, however, on the same night Moonraker was backed heavily at 120*l*. to 100*l*. and on subsequent days similar odds, and even 5 to 4, were laid. Still Grimaldi had strong friends, and was heavily backed at evens, and in some cases was the favorite at 6 to 4, conditionally on Mr. Osbaldeston's riding.

Both horses were allowed to be in excellent condition, and 'nothing the worse' for their Thursday's exertion. Grimaldi had a decided advantage in youth and freshness, and came up from Warwickshire with an excellent character. He is twelve years old, by Grimaldi, out of Miss Bab, by Highland-fling, out of Lady Bab, and bred by Mr. Clifford, of Gloucestershire. By Mr. Clifford he was sold, at four years old, to Mr. Wynnet; by that gentleman sold to Mr. Bray, and from Mr. Bray he came into the hands of Mr. Evans. His colour is grey. Moonraker is what is called a 'dark' horse; that is to say, neither his sire nor dam is known. He was originally bought, we believe, at 35 guineas; and, after doing some excellent work, was again sold for 80 guineas. He was sent up from Warwickshire as nothing but a 'good un', although he had seen an immense deal of service; and his fame was established by winning two steeple races in succession, in the neighbourhood of St. Albans, which was followed up by his third victory on Thursday week. His colour is bay, but his age is not known. He is a high-couraged horse, strong and willing in a heavy country, and an excellent fencer; stopping at nothing, and taking his leaps with uncommon clearness and precision. The distance agreed to be run was four miles, the precise ground to be chosen by the umpires–Colonel Charitie on the part of Moonraker; and Mr. Meyrick, on the part of Grimaldi. On Monday it was known that both horses were near the appointed place–Moonraker, at Mr. Elmore's farm, near Harrow; and Grimaldi at Neasdon. It was mutually agreed that the riders should meet at Mr. Elmore's to weigh, at two o'clock.

In the course of the morning the umpires met and proceeded to select the course which was finally fixed to be from a field on Mr. Copeland's farm, near the seven-mile stone, on the Edgware-road, down a gradual descent across a flat country, at the foot of Harrow Hill, into a field in front of a Mr. Hawkins's, a farm-house, at Harrow Weald. The fences were by no means difficult, and the ground, although heavy (principally meadow or pasture), partook more, as was remarked by some old fielders, of the character of a race course than a laborious hunting country, and therefore more favorable, in their opinion, for Grimaldi, who was supposed to possess more speed than strength. The approaches to the scene of action presented a lively spectacle during the forenoon. The roads were thronged with vehicles of every description and an immense body of horsemen, who spread themselves in all directions over the fields, breaking down hedges and rendering the small leaps there still more easy. Harrow was overflowing, and here innumerable groups waited till the news arrived of the precise route to be taken. All then proceeded to take up the stations best calculated to afford a view of the contest. The principal body of the spectators concentrated in the neighbourhood of Mr. Hawkins's farm, keeping the winning flag in view.

Subsequent to the ground being chosen, the stakes were said to be all right, that is to say, each umpire held his friend's cash in his own hands: rather an unusual way of making stakes good. It was now universally known that Mr. Osbaldeston would ride Grimaldi, and Mr. Seffert, Moonraker–but, after a long delay beyond the hour appointed, which occurred before Mr. Osbaldeston reached Mr. Elmore's farm, apprehensions began to be entertained that the race would not come off. These fears were dissipated by the arrival of Mr. Osbaldeston and his friends, and all now became anxious for the commencement of the sport. Previous to this, the flags had been carried towards the starting post–Mr. Seffert having ridden a short distance to see them placed. This act of Mr. Seffert having been communicated to Mr. Osbaldeston, that gentleman concluded that Mr. Seffert had seen the whole line of the intended struggle, and therefore insisted on having an equal advantage. This led to some dispute, which ended in an agreement that both should go over the ground; and they accordingly, contrary to all precedent in steeple chases, set off on their hacks attended by a cloud of equestrians, over hedge and ditch to Harrow Weald – an experiment which afforded no small amusement to the outlying spectators, from the numerous accidents and unseemly prostrations which were presented to their view. On reaching the last field, it did not seem that the precise goal, or winning point, had been stipulated; a hedge leading to a paddock next the farm was named, but to this Mr. Osbaldeston objected, on the ground that Steeple Chases generally ended in the middle of a field, and not in an abrupt leap. This matter was soon adjusted by naming a small drain or gutter in the centre of the meadow, as the final 'scratch', the first horse over this gutter to be considered the winner, and two flags

136. *The First Steeplechase on Record* by Henry Alken, engraved by J. Harris: Plate 2 of a series of four published in 1839. The steeplechase, which took place in 1803, was an impromptu race arranged by cavalry officers posted at Ipswich barracks. With their nightshirts over their uniforms, they rode at midnight from Ipswich to nearby Nacton Church.

having been planted so as to render this more distinct. By these delays much time was wasted, and the hour of four instead of one, the original hour for starting mentioned, had arrived to the infinite annoyance of those pedestrians who had been lounging backwards and forwards over the damp earth, and any thing but desirable or gallant towards many of the fair sex, who, seated in open carriages, exposed to no friendly breeze, waited the event with their customary patience.

At last, the preliminary view being completed, the riders and their partizans returned to Mr. Elmore's farm, again showing their skill or clumsiness in their progress; and here it is due to state, that in the most difficult leaps the palm of superiority was deservedly given to a young and beautiful lady, whose graceful seat, perfect confidence, and unshrinking courage, often put her followers to the blush—blushes which were occasionally hidden by that natural paint of which the surrounding ditches afforded abundance.

At length the important ceremony of weighing took place, and the horses were sent to the starting post. Mr. Osbaldeston had but little to add to his ordinary weight to reach the stipulated amount of 11 st. 7 lbs., while Mr. Seffert had nearly sixteen pounds of 'dead weight' attached round his loins in belts. Both wore silk jackets and jockey caps. It was after five o'clock before they mounted and prepared for the race. In the interim the whole line they had to take had been marked by flags at convenient distances. The dusk of evening, with a slight fog, had supplanted the previous brightness of the day, and many had actually quitted the ground giving up all hope of their promised amusement. At last the word was given, and off went the competitors at a slashing speed. Moonraker took the lead—Grimaldi, as had been previously announced by Mr. Osbaldeston, waiting close upon him. About a mile and a half or two miles from the starting-post, Mr. Seffert, after taking his leap, swerved towards a stile, but again cut in, making an angle. Mr. Osbaldeston, on the contrary, kept the direct line, and, he says, accidentally came in contact with Mr. Seffert as he again took up his straight running. We are informed that Mr. Seffert complained of this, and exclaimed, that whatever was the result of the race, he should mention the fact. He then went on, still waited on by Grimaldi, till within half a mile of home, where, after crossing a fence, he went towards a gate, expecting to get a more direct line for the destined goal—while Mr. Osbaldeston quickened his speed, and dashed straight forward. Mr. Seffert found he was mistaken, and again got into the field with Mr. Osbaldeston, who had, by Mr. Seffert's error, got nearly a hundred yards a-head. Every nerve of Moonraker was now urged to its utmost to regain the lost ground; but

from henceforth his chance was lost. Grimaldi had got the lead, and kept it—and in coming through a gap in the corner of the last field, his success was put beyond a doubt. Moonraker followed, evidently much distressed, but incapable of additional exertion. Mr. Seffert seemed rather to support than to push his steed; and seeing Grimaldi cross the 'rubicon', he pulled up—Grimaldi being pronounced by acclamation the winner by several lengths.

Objection to the Stakes being given up.—All parties, as by previous agreement, next returned to Mr. Elmore's farm—towards which the horses were led —and here, on the umpires being called, Mr. Seffert preferred his complaint of having been ridden against by Mr. Osbaldeston, and appealed to Mr. Osbaldeston whether that had been the case. Mr. Osbaldeston, we understand, admitted the fact, but stated most distinctly that he could not avoid it—it was perfectly accidental, and solely arising from the angle which Mr. Seffert had made.

Mr. Elmore said he had no desire to make a wrangle, or to object unnecessarily to the stakes being given up; nevertheless, as his rider had made the complaint, he would leave it in his hands and to the umpires to come to that decision which seemed to them most consistent with justice to all parties.

The stakeholder, having heard both sides, said he deemed it necessary to hear further evidence, and, before he gave up the stakes, to submit the question to the Jockey Club.

It was six o'clock before the race was concluded, and nearly three quarters of an hour elapsed before the carriages congregated in the lane leading to Mr. Hawkins's farm could be extricated. To the spectators the day was fatiguing and vexatious, and general complaints were made of the want of that regularity which the importance of the match demanded, as well as the twaddling disputes which arose, and led to such unreasonable delay. This delay was not without its benefit, however, as it rendered the leaps mere trifles.

Among the distinguished persons whom we saw on the ground were Lord Errol, Lord Abercorn, Lord Rivers, Count D'Orsq, Lord Clonbrock, Lord Grimstone, Colonel Peel, Colonel Anson, L. Charlton Esq. –. Ramsay, Esq., MP, together with some of the most celebrated persons on the Turf.

Meeting of the Umpires—On Wednesday, Colonel Meyrick, Colonel Charitie, Mr. Osbaldeston, and Mr. Elmore, had a meeting upon the subject in dispute, when it was mutually agreed to refer the matter to Colonel Anson, to whom the evidence was submitted; and on the same evening he declared, at Tattersall's, that he saw no reason for an objection

137. The racehorse Jerry, by J. Herring, c. 1825. The son of Smolensko, foaled in 1821, and pictured here with his jockey, J. Smith. Jerry's most notable achievements were victories in the 1824 York and Doncaster St. Legers.

to the stakes being given up; but, on the contrary, was of opinion, that Mr. Osbaldeston had fairly won, and was entitled to all the advantages of his victory. This of course, sets the matter at rest.

SKATING

A TIME OF RAPTURE

From *The Prelude* by William Wordsworth, 1850

And in the frosty season, when the sun
Was set, and visible for many a mile
The cottage windows blazed through twilight gloom,
I heeded not their summons: happy time
It was indeed for all of us–for me
It was a time of rapture! Clear and loud
The village clock tolled six–I wheeled about
Proud and exulting like an untired horse
That cares not for his home. All shod with steel,
We hissed along the polished ice in games
Confederate, imitative of the chase
And woodland pleasures–the resounding horn,
The pack loud chiming, and the hunted hare,
So through the darkness and the cold we flew,
And now a voice was idle; with the din
Smitten, the precipices rang aloud;
The leafless trees and every icy crag
Tinkled like iron; while far distant hills
Into the tumult sent an alien sound
Of melancholy not unnoticed, while the stars
Eastward were sparkling clear, and in the west
The orange sky of evening died away.

HOW THE PICKWICKIANS DISPORTED THEMSELVES UPON THE ICE

From *Pickwick Papers* by Charles Dickens, 1836

'Now,' said Wardle, after a substantial lunch, with the agreeable items of strong beer and cherry-brandy, had been done ample justice to, 'what say you to an hour on the ice? We shall have plenty of time.'

'Capital!' said Mr. Benjamin Allen.

'Prime!' ejaculated Mr. Bob Sawyer.

'You skait of course, Winkle?' said Wardle.

'Ye—yes: oh yes'; replied Mr. Winkle. 'I—I—am rather out of practice.'

'Oh, do skait, Mr. Winkle,' said Arabella. 'I like to see it so much.'

'Oh, it is so graceful,' said another young lady.

A third young lady said it was elegant, and a fourth expressed her opinion that it was 'swan-like.'

138. Winter amusement, c. 1852.

when old Wardle and Benjamin Allen, assisted by the aforesaid Bob Sawyer, performed some mystic evolutions which they called a reel.

All this time, Mr. Winkle, with his face and hands blue with the cold, had been forcing a gimlet into the soles of his feet, and putting his skaits on, with the points behind, and getting the straps into a very complicated and entangled state, with the assistance of Mr. Snodgrass, who knew rather less about skaits than a Hindoo. At length, however, with the assistance of Mr. Weller, the unfortunate skaits were firmly screwed and buckled on, and Mr. Winkle was raised to his feet.

'Now, then, sir,' said Sam, in an encouraging tone; 'off with you, and show 'em how to do it.'

'Stop, Sam, stop!' said Mr. Winkle, trembling violently, and clutching hold of Sam's arms with the grasp of a drowning man. 'How slippery it is, Sam!'

'Not an uncommon thing upon ice, sir,' replied Mr. Weller. 'Hold up, sir!'

This last observation of Mr. Weller's bore reference to a demonstration Mr. Winkle made at the instant, of a frantic desire to throw his feet in the air, and dash the back of his head on the ice.

'These—these—are very awkward skaits; ain't they, Sam?' inquired Mr. Winkle, staggering.

'I'm afeerd there's an orkard gen'l'm'n in 'em, sir,' replied Sam.

'Now, Winkle,' cried Mr. Pickwick, quite unconscious that there was anything the matter. 'Come; the ladies are all anxiety.'

'Yes, yes,' replied Mr. Winkle, with a ghastly smile, 'I'm coming.'

'Just goin' to begin,' said Sam, endeavouring to disengage himself. 'Now, sir, start off!'

'Stop an instant, Sam,' gasped Mr. Winkle, clinging most affectionately to Mr. Weller. 'I find I've got a couple of coats at home, that I don't want, Sam. You may have them, Sam.'

'Thank'ee, sir,' replied Mr. Weller.

'Never mind touching your hat, Sam,' said Mr. Winkle, hastily. 'You needn't take your hand away to do that. I meant to have given you five shillings this morning for a Christmas-box, Sam. I'll give it you this afternoon, Sam.'

'You're werry good, sir,' replied Mr. Weller.

'Just hold me at first, Sam; will you?' said Mr. Winkle. 'There—that's right. I shall soon get in the way of it, Sam. Not too fast, Sam; not too fast.'

Mr. Winkle, stepping forward with his body half doubled up, was being assisted over the ice by Mr. Weller in a very singular and un-swan-like manner, when Mr. Pickwick most innocently shouted from the

'I should be very happy, I'm sure,' said Mr. Winkle, reddening; 'but I have no skaits.'

This objection was at once overruled. Trundle had a couple of pairs, and the fat boy announced that there were half-a-dozen more downstairs; whereat Mr. Winkle expressed exquisite delight, and looked exquisitely uncomfortable.

Old Wardle led the way to a pretty large sheet of ice; and the fat boy and Mr. Weller having shovelled and swept away the snow which had fallen on it during the night, Mr. Bob Sawyer adjusted his skaits with a dexterity which to Mr. Winkle was perfectly marvellous and described circles with his left leg, and cut figures of eight, and inscribed upon the ice, without once stopping for breath, a great many other pleasant and astonishing devices, to the excessive satisfaction of Mr. Pickwick, Mr. Tupman, and the ladies: which reached a pitch of positive enthusiasm,

139. Skaters on the Serpentine in London, by Thomas Rowlandson, 1786.

opposite bank:

'Sam!'

'Sir?' said Mr. Weller.

'Here. I want you.'

'Let go, sir,' said Sam. 'Don't you hear the governor a-callin'? Let go, sir.'

With a violent effort, Mr. Weller disengaged himself from the grasp of the agonised Pickwickian; and, in so doing, administered a considerable impetus to the unhappy Mr. Winkle. With an accuracy which no degree of dexterity or practice could have insured, that unfortunate gentleman bore swiftly down into the centre of the reel, at the very moment when Mr. Bob Sawyer was performing a flourish of unparalleled beauty. Mr. Winkle struck wildly against him, and with a loud crash they both fell heavily down. Mr. Pickwick ran to the spot. Bob Sawyer had risen to his feet, but Mr. Winkle was far too wise to do anything of the kind, in skaits. He was seated on the ice, making spasmodic efforts to smile; but anguish was depicted on every lineament of his countenance.

'Are you hurt?' inquired Mr. Benjamin Allen, with great anxiety.

'Not much,' said Mr. Winkle, rubbing his back very hard.

'I wish you'd let me bleed you,' said Mr. Benjamin with great eagerness.

'No, thank you,' replied Mr. Winkle hurriedly.

'I really think you had better,' said Allen.

'Thank you,' replied Mr. Winkle; 'I'd rather not.'

'What do you think, Mr. Pickwick?' inquired Bob Sawyer.

Mr. Pickwick was excited and indignant. He beckoned to Mr. Weller, and said in a stern voice, 'Take his skaits off.'

'No; but really I had scarcely begun,' remonstrated Mr. Winkle.

'Take his skaits off,' repeated Mr. Pickwick firmly.

The command was not to be resisted. Mr. Winkle allowed Sam to obey it, in silence.

'Lift him up,' said Mr. Pickwick. Sam assisted him to rise.

Mr. Pickwick retired a few paces apart from the by-standers; and, beckoning his friend to approach, fixed a searching look upon him, and uttered in a low, but distinct and emphatic tone these words:

'You're a humbug, sir.'

'A what!' said Mr. Winkle, staring.

'A humbug, sir. I will speak plainer, if you wish it. An impostor, sir.'

With these words, Mr. Pickwick turned slowly on his heel, and rejoined his friends.

While Mr. Pickwick was delivering himself of the sentiment just recorded, Mr. Weller and the fat boy, having by their joint endeavours

cut out a slide, were exercising themselves thereupon, in a very masterly and brilliant manner. Sam Weller, in particular, was displaying that beautiful feat of fancy sliding which is currently denominated 'knocking at the cobbler's door,' and which is achieved by skimming over the ice on one foot, and occasionally giving a twopenny postman's knock upon it with the other. It was a good long slide, and there was something in the motion which Mr. Pickwick, who was very cold with standing still, could not help envying.

'It looks a nice warm exercise that, doesn't it?' he inquired of Wardle, when that gentleman was thoroughly out of breath, by reason of the indefatigable manner in which he had converted his legs into a pair of compasses, and drawn complicated problems on the ice.

'Ah, it does, indeed,' replied Wardle. 'Do you slide?'

'I used to do so, on the gutters, when I was a boy,' replied Mr. Pickwick.

'Try it now,' said Wardle.

'Oh do, please, Mr. Pickwick,' cried all the ladies.

'I should be very happy to afford you any amusement,' replied Mr. Pickwick, 'but I haven't done such a thing these thirty years.'

'Pooh! pooh! nonsense!' said Wardle, dragging off his skaits with the impetuosity which characterised all his proceedings. 'Here; I'll keep you company; come along.' And away went the good-tempered old fellow down the slide, with a rapidity which came very close upon Mr. Weller, and beat the fat boy all to nothing.

Mr. Pickwick paused, considered, pulled off his gloves and put them in his hat; took two or three short runs; baulked himself as often: and at last took another run, and went slowly and gravely down the slide, with his feet about a yard and a quarter apart; amidst the gratified shouts of all the spectators.

'Keep the pot a bilin', sir!' said Sam; and down went Wardle again, and then Mr. Pickwick, and then Sam, and then Mr. Winkle, and then Mr. Bob Sawyer, and then the fat boy, and then Mr. Snodgrass, following closely upon each other's heels, and running after each other with as much eagerness as if all their future prospects in life depended on their expedition.

It was the most intensely interesting thing, to observe the manner in which Mr. Pickwick performed his share in the ceremony; to watch the torture of anxiety with which he viewed the person behind, gaining upon him at the imminent hazard of tripping him up: to see him gradually expend the painful force which he had put on at first, and turn slowly round on the slide, with his face towards the point from which he had started: to contemplate the playful smile which mantled on his face when

140. Skaters, c. 1848.

125

he had accomplished the distance, and the eagerness with which he turned round when he had done so, and ran after his predecessor: his black gaiters tripping pleasantly through the snow, and his eyes beaming cheerfulness and gladness through his spectacles. And when he was knocked down (which happened upon the average every third round), it was the most invigorating sight that can possibly be imagined, to behold him gather up his hat, gloves, and handkerchief, with a glowing countenance, and resume his station in the rank, with an ardour and enthusiasm that nothing could abate.

TENNIS

THE KING ON COURT

From Samuel Pepys's Diary, 1659-99

From him I went to see a great match at tennis, between Prince Rupert and one Captaine Cooke, against Bab. May and the elder Chichly; where the King was, and Court; and it seems they are the best players at tennis in the nation. But this puts me in mind of what I observed in the morning, that the King, playing at tennis, had a steelyard carried to him; and I was told it was to weigh him after he had done playing; and at noon Mr. Ashburnham told me that it is only the King's curiosity, which he usually hath of weighing himself before and after his play, to see how much he loses in weight by playing; and this day he lost $4\frac{1}{2}$ lbs.

PARKER'S PIECE

From Cambridge Review May 1891 by James Kenneth Stephen

To see good Tennis! what diviner joy
Can fill our leisure, or our minds employ?
Not Sylvia's self is more supremely fair,
Than balls that hurtle through the conscious air.
Not Stella's form instinct with truer grace

Than Lambert's racket poised to win the chase.
Not Chloe's harp more native to the ear,
Than the tense strings which smite the flying sphere.

When Lambert boasts the superhuman force,
Or splite the echoing grille without remorse;
When Harraine, as graceful as of yore,
Wins better than a yard, upon the floor;
When Alfred's ringing cheer proclaims success,
Or Saunders volleys in resistlessness;
When Heathcote's service makes the dedans ring,
With just applause, and own its honoured king;
When Pettitt's prowess all our zeal awoke
Till high Olympus shuddered at the stroke;
Or when, receiving thirty and the floor,
The novice serves a dozen faults or more;
Or some plump don, perspiring and profane,
Assails the roof and breaks the exalted pane;
When vantage, five games all, the door is called,
And Europe pauses, breathless and appalled,
Till lo! the ball by cunning hand caressed
Finds in the winning gallery a nest;
These are the moments, this the bliss supreme,
Which makes the artist's joy, the poet's dream.

Let cricketers await the tardy sun,
Break one another's shins and call it fun;
Let Scotia's golfers through the affrighted land
With crooked knee and glaring eyeball stand;
Let football rowdies show their straining thews,
And tell their triumphs to a mud-stained Muse;
Let indiarubber pellets dance on grass
Where female arts the ruder sex surpass;
Let other people play at other things;
The king of games is still the game of kings.

141. A tennis match between Mr. A. Lyttleton and Mr. C. Saunders at the reopening of the Princes Club, Brighton by the Prince of Wales in 1893.

TEXT ILLUSTRATIONS
AND ACKNOWLEDGEMENTS

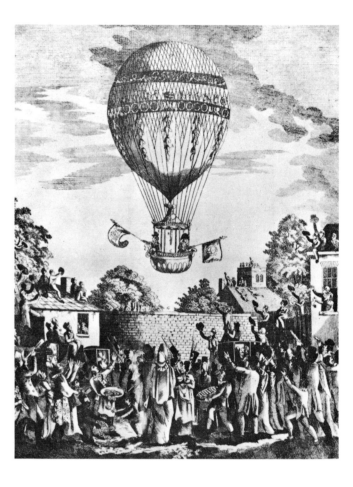

142. Mr. Sadler and Capt. Paget, R.N.
ascending from the gardens of the
Mermaid Tavern at Hackney on
August 12th, 1811.